The Nonprofit Secret

The Nonprofit Secret

The Six Principles of Successful Board/CEO Partnerships

Jonathan D. Schick

The Nonprofit Secret
The Six Principles of Successful Board/CEO Partnerships

© 2009 Jonathan Schick

Manufactured in the United States of America.

For information, please contact:

The P3 Press
16200 North Dallas Parkway, Suite 170
Dallas, Texas 75248

www.thep3press.com

972-381-0009

A New Era in Publishing™

ISBN-13: 978-1-933651-41-5
ISBN-10: 1-933651-41-5
LCCN: 2009902621

Author contact information:

Jonathan D. Schick

jds@goalconsulting.com

www.goalconsulting.com

To Aliza, Nachi, Aaron, Moshe, and Yehuda,
may you succeed as the child
succeeds the father.

Contents

Acknowledgments ix
Memo to the CEO and the Board xi
The Six Principles of Successful Board/CEO Partnerships xvii

Principle I
The Board Focuses on Governance, Not Management 1

Principle II
The Board Has One Employee: the CEO. 19

Principle III
The CEO Has Only One Employer:
the Board as a Whole 31

Principle IV
The Board Creates Committees to Help
Accomplish Its Own Job, Not the CEO's 45

Principle V
The Board Evaluates Its CEO through an Executive
Support and Appraisal Team (ESAT). 65

Principle VI
The Board Conducts Its Own Annual Self-Appraisal 83

The Next Step. 97
Appendix A: CEO SPAN 104
Appendix B: Six Principles at a Glance. 113

Acknowledgments

It's hard to know where to start in offering thanks to the many friends, family, and colleagues who have supported me and this project since the very beginning some seven years ago:

My dear children, for whom I dedicated the book as a guidepost as they head to adulthood and the challenges of life.

My grandparents, of blessed memory, who gave me their independent streak combined with a natty resilience. My grandfather, who authored *Joseph's Harvest*, an ethical tome, in 1933, served as an invisible yet palpable inspiration.

My parents who, besides giving me life, have given me tremendous tools along with a nice-sized helping of worry as a perennial motivator.

My four siblings who, though we are geographically separate, have been supportive in many different ways. My in-laws and sisters/brothers-in-law who have been a great second family. Many aunts, uncles, and cousins who have been instrumental at important times in my life.

My close friends through the years in Dallas, Boston, Jerusalem, New York, Washington, Rochester, New Haven, and in the dark spaces where you let light in.

My students through the years, at the adult, university, high school, and even grade school level, who have provided much to my own development as an educator, speaker, consultant, and human being.

My many colleagues, advisors, and mentors, who, since I started my consultancy back in 2003, have been amazing friends, cheerleaders, and repositories of wisdom and good counsel. You have left your imprint on this book.

My outstanding clients in the great state of Texas and throughout the United States and Canada, and specifically the ones who agreed to contribute vignettes or quotes in the book. You are the reason this book has come to life in so many vibrant colors.

The group of ten reviewers who provided invaluable recommendations, many of which are reflected in the final text. Thanks so much for your time and expertise.

The team of professionals who were involved with this book at many different levels. You are the behind-the-scenes reason that this book is a reality.

My dear wife who has been an incredible pillar of strength throughout these years. Thank you for believing in me.

And to God, who kept with me through thick and thin and who, through His compassion and love, has allowed this day to come.

Memo to the CEO[1] and the Board

If you've picked up this book, chances are you're either intimately acquainted with the nonprofit world or you would like to be. As a board member, CEO, staff member, volunteer, or donor, you are providing a service that makes a genuine difference in people's lives. As you undoubtedly know, your ability to provide that service is highly dependent on the people at the helm of your organization. The way the board and the CEO communicate and interact with one another will shape not only the inner dynamics of your organization but also the services you provide to the community at large.

After many years of working with nonprofits, I've unlocked the secret to maintaining a thriving, healthy organization. The secret is not policy, it isn't all about fundraising, and it doesn't directly concern your strategic plan. While those things are important, it's actually much simpler than that. At the heart of every successful nonprofit is one thing: the board/CEO partnership. And at the heart of a successful partnership between the board and the CEO is an effective and ethical system of governance.

---

1. Your nonprofit might call the executive by a different name; for example, you may use the title Executive Director, President, or Head. Though the titles are interchangeable, for the sake of consistency I'll refer to the executive as CEO throughout this book.

When it comes to nonprofit governance, some people have the attitude that "If you've seen one board, you've seen just one board"—meaning that there's no systemic way of governing. The nonprofit arena often becomes highly political, and since people are people, there's really nothing that can be done about it; every nonprofit must deal with the vagaries of its particular board. But while each board will naturally have idiosyncrasies, there *is* a system that works across the board. A system that's simple, clear, and powerful. A system about real and lasting change. A system that will allow you to make a meaningful shift in the entire culture of your organization, unleashing the full potential of your board. A system that unlocks the nonprofit secret, equipping your nonprofit with the tools it needs today to change the shape of tomorrow.

That system is called the Six Principles of Successful Board/CEO Partnerships.

I've witnessed the Six Principles work their magic over and over again in a variety of settings, including nonprofit organizations, government agencies, and private schools. One CEO reported that after her organization chose to adopt the Six Principles model, the average gift of $1,850 per trustee spiked to an average gift of $10,250. That's a 450 percent increase. Another CEO told me that as a result of our work together, they had experienced a striking crescendo in board participation. Whereas before they had only averaged three hours of strategic governance activity per year, it had leapt to twenty-six hours—a 760 percent increase! That's the kind of culture change that has real and long-lasting results for an organization.

When people discover the simplest, but often overlooked, keys to strong board/CEO relationships, all kinds of exciting things start to happen. I've watched the Six Principles model revolutionize the governance culture for a variety of nonprofits that run the gamut in size, type, structure, and mission, with budgets ranging from eighty thousand dollars to eighteen million. Once implemented, the model works to improve communication skills and foster an atmosphere of trust, collaboration, and risk-taking. It ends the stress and fear typically associated with evaluation through the ESAT (Executive Support & Appraisal Team) system. It introduces SPAN (Strategic Performance Appraisal & Navigation) as a way for board and committee members, CEOs, and staff to effectively set goals and evaluate their own performance. It energizes and empowers board members by enabling each of them to play a proactive role. And because of its culture-changing capacities, the Six Principles model builds consensus and morale among stakeholders, enabling organizations to rise above the specific challenges unique to their environment.

I created the Six Principles as a deeply personal response to the unique challenges of the nonprofit world. The system draws strongly from my own experiences as both an executive and a board member. As the founding CEO of two nonprofits, I experienced two very different types of boards. One had a hands-off board, and at times I struggled to engage them and had the challenge of initiating action. At the other, an invested, managing board, I had to construct an appropriate perimeter between the board and staff. When I started out, one of my earliest mistakes was that I didn't insist on my own evaluation. Because of this, I experienced the effects of not having an effective system of appraisal, and I witnessed firsthand the amorphous type of structure each board was struggling under. Later, as a board member of several other nonprofit organizations, including serving as the chair of an international academy, I experienced the other end of the spectrum. That's when I came to appreciate the distinctive set of worries and woes that boards face.

Over the years I've watched friends and colleagues suffer from a general lack of process and structure as board members. I've witnessed countless new trustees join a board flush with high hopes and good intentions, only to quickly become frustrated by their seeming inability to enact real and lasting change in their organizations. So many times I've seen the consequences of the absence of an effective governance model, which is often joined by a pervasive misunderstanding of how the board and CEO were meant to work alongside one another. This lack of structure has repeatedly resulted in abandoned hopes, lost jobs, and atrophied dreams.

After I began my consulting business, I worked with hundreds of clients who dealt daily with these tough realities. Most of the time, things didn't go wrong because of any one disgruntled person trying to run the rest off course. I typically found that people simply didn't know what they were supposed to do. Board members and CEOs alike were sophisticated and well-intentioned, but they misunderstood the process because they had never really internalized it. As my work unfolded, I realized that it was the partnership between the board and the CEO that ultimately defined whether or not an organization was healthy and successful. At their core, the Six Principles are about growing the relationship between your organization's board and CEO into a significantly more effective union.

As a whole, the Six Principles form a model of ethical governance that is revolutionary in its utter simplicity. I've taken all the essentials of good governance theory and practice and distilled them into six principles that, if used correctly, can cause a powerful change in the culture of your organization. Note that it's the Six Principles of *Successful Board/CEO Partnerships*, not the Six Principles of *Successful Boards*—the partnership is the key. Both arms of your organization must be willing to accept and implement this new model. One branch can be coasting along smoothly, but if it's not working in harmony with the other side, your organization simply isn't going to function at its fullest potential. When the board and CEO are working in tandem, you'll experience a burst of possibility that you never imagined possible. By helping you find ways to use your people's energies in a positive and affirming way, your organization will achieve unprecedented success.

This book is broken down into six clear chapters, each chapter devoted to one of the Six Principles. To better illuminate the comprehensive journey an organization must take to achieve better board governance, we'll follow the story of one particular nonprofit as they implement the Six Principles model. This organization and its cast of characters are fictional, but their journey is very real. They are a composite of many of my clients, bold and perceptive people who were willing to change the way their nonprofit operated by strengthening the pivotal relationship between board and executive. In so doing, they were able to change the organization itself.

You'll also have the opportunity to witness how each principle has affected actual change: I've included various stories gleaned from my real life experiences of working alongside nonprofits. Many of my former clients have contributed anecdotes and comments regarding how the Six Principles changed the culture in their organizations, helping them establish a strong focus on ethical governance and lasting growth.

Now it's your turn. No matter if you are a first time board member, a seasoned trustee, a veteran CEO, a newly christened executive, or simply passionate about nonprofits—this book was written for you. And whether you're part of a museum, environmental group, professional association, government agency, school, foundation, advocacy group, hospital, faith-based organization, social services agency, or any other type of nonprofit, it's time to unlock the secret of the Six Principles for your organization. If you do, you'll reap the many rewards. This book will show you how.

Jonathan D. Schick, President
GOAL Consulting

The Six Principles of Successful Board/CEO Partnerships

Principle I

The board focuses on governance, not management. Effective nonprofit boards empower their CEOs to run their agencies. In other words, board members establish the desired outcomes while enabling the CEO to determine the methods. The board neither micromanages nor rubber stamps. Rather, successful boards spend their time focusing on fundamental issues and major policy decisions.

Principle II

The board has one employee: the CEO. A basic tenet of governance is that the board hires the CEO who in turn hires all the other staff. The board views the CEO's role as similar to one of a corporate executive; thus, all accountability rests upon the CEO alone. For instance, the board would not hold the marketing director answerable for low event turnout; the CEO alone is responsible to the board.

Principle III

The CEO has only one employer: the board as a whole. A board that ethically governs makes it known that the CEO is responsible only to the unified board. Thus, the CEO is not faced with the political pressure of fielding the special interests of individual trustees. Likewise, board members understand that their collective responsibility takes precedence over their individual relationships with the CEO.

Principle IV

The board creates committees to help accomplish its own job, not the CEO's. The board does not create committees to direct the day-to-day management of the agency. Essentially, committees such as program or personnel are duplicative of the managerial duties assigned to the CEO. In addition, these committees compromise the board's duty to speak as a cohesive unit. Conversely, the board should create committees to help with its own responsibilities, for example: a governance committee, a finance committee, and an ESAT.

Principle V

The board evaluates its CEO through an Executive Support and Appraisal Team. This committee is charged by the board to jointly establish the CEO's annual and long-term performance goals. These objectives are based on the agency's annual agenda and are firmly rooted in its mission. The ESAT meets with the CEO during the year to assess progress and then, at year's end, reports its findings to the greater board. Under this model, the board engages the CEO in a proactive and ethical evaluation process.

Principle VI

The board conducts its own annual self-appraisal. After a board is trained and educated in this governance model, the board appraises its efficacy on a yearly basis. Board members have a fiduciary responsibility to the agency and its constituency to assure that their roles and responsibilities are being carried out appropriately and productively. A board that strategically appraises its CEO and concurrently appraises itself sends a powerful message to the community.

Principle I

The Board Focuses on Governance, Not Management

Early October

Invitation Meltdown in the Boardroom

For Teresa Thompson, every day with her nine-year-old daughter is a blessing. Today, Rebecca is healthy, strong, and fully enjoying the fourth grade. But just a few short years ago, Rebecca was engaged in a life-or-death struggle with leukemia that shook the foundations of Teresa's world.

When Rebecca was first diagnosed, Teresa was too grief-stricken to seek support outside her family. But after six hard months, Teresa took a huge step and began volunteering for *Life with Leukemia*, a nonprofit organization that provides educational and personalized support for young leukemia patients and their families. As Rebecca slowly got healthier, Teresa dedicated more time to the organization, and after a year of impassioned work, she was asked to be a member of the board of directors. She gratefully accepted and has served on the board for the last two years.

But lately, Teresa has been feeling frustrated and confused about her role in the organization. Every November, *Life with Leukemia* throws a grand-scale benefit dinner at an area hotel, and this year Teresa has been elected to head up the Planning Committee. One of the other committee members designed a colorful invitation that, in Teresa's opinion, is inappropriate and garish. Because of the impact *Life with Leukemia* has had on her own life, Teresa feels the invitations should have a more personal feel; her idea was to feature a picture of a child the organization has helped. Unfortunately, the difference of opinion has blown into a full-scale disagreement, and the whole board has spent the last two meetings arguing over the invitations. Teresa strongly believes in the organization and what it stands for, but she feels like her opinions aren't being heard or valued. And because she feels responsible for pulling the whole board off track, she's struggling over whether or not she should submit her resignation.

Just a few months ago, the *Life with Leukemia* board was a healthy, functioning team committed to upholding the organization's mission. What went wrong?

The answer is simple: they started to micromanage.

At the core of a successful board/CEO partnership is Principle I of the Six Principles: the board focuses on governance, not management. Effective nonprofit boards establish the desired outcomes and then empower their CEOs to establish the methods for reaching them. The board should neither micromanage—like Life with Leukemia started to do—nor rubber stamp without any real engagement. Rather, the board should spend its time focusing on fundamental issues and major policy decisions.

Teresa's dilemma isn't unique. Boards often begin to take on staff roles, especially at nonprofits with a limited number of employees. But it's not a board member's job to design an event invitation, and the issue certainly shouldn't take up valuable meeting time. Debating management issues creates unnecessary strife and destroys focus. It diverts the board from what it should be focusing on, and instead makes members feel devalued and divided. Similarly, when boards have no real impact on the nonprofits they serve, members begin to feel disempowered and disillusioned. So many nonprofit boards swing between the two extremes, often missing their one true purpose: to govern the organization.

So how does a nonprofit board remain within the boundaries of governance? What kinds of things should be left to the CEO, and which duties belong to the board?

The Board Engagement Matrix

Below is a basic diagram called the Board Engagement Matrix. The Matrix divides the work of an organization into five categories, beginning with the fundamental and ending with the procedural. The degree of the board's engagement should decrease with each category, following the downward slope of an inverted cone.

Actions	Issues	Examples	Amount of Board Engagement
Fundamental	Mission and identity	Considering a merger with another agency. Expanding geographical service area.	
Primary	Relationship of departments to overall mission	Launching a capital campaign. Evaluation of CEO.	
Tactical	Processes such as planning, budgeting, etc.	Program adoption. Annual planning of budget.	
Operative	Decisions regarding day-to-day practices	Volunteer reimbursement policy. Staff absentee policy.	
Procedural	Procedures which handle routine transactions	Scheduling of events. Dress code.	

This is a visual way of looking at the division between governance and management. Where should board members be spending their time? If you look at the top of the matrix, you'll see that issues of mission and identity are the board's top priority. If you are on the board of a national agency, for example, and you hire a new CEO, you're not going to leave it up to him or her alone to decide whether you should expand your boundaries to become an international organization. That's a board-level decision. You'll get input from your CEO, of course, but the ultimate decision falls under the fundamental responsibilities of a board.

At the other end of the spectrum are procedural and operative concerns. Most nonprofit board members can relate to the agony of tedious board meetings where big picture issues are drowned out by the organization's day-to-day minutiae. How many times have you spent half a board meeting discussing transactional issues, event scheduling, dress code, or a staff absentee policy? While these issues are certainly important, they have nothing to do with governance—they fall under the management umbrella. And when a board spends over an hour discussing who's going to cut the ribbon at an opening ceremony, it's no wonder that members walk out the door feeling utterly deflated, all their energy sapped.

In many years of working with nonprofits, I've hardly ever encountered a board that's suffering from a lack of commitment on the part of its members. Usually, people genuinely care about the organization and are dedicated to it, eager to offer their unique talents and gifts. In much the same way, it's rarely the case that one bad egg is causing all the board's problems. Of the organizations I've worked with, I would estimate only 5–10 percent can trace the bulk of their problems to a particularly toxic board member or CEO, someone completely consumed by self-interest. Typically, people become board members because they want to help. And all too often, they start out brimming with energy and idealism, ready to take an active role, only to discover that the board's governing responsibilities are inextricably blurred with the management duties of the CEO.

When a board strays from a firm focus on governance, several things can happen. Instead of each individual's skills being put to good use, their energies lie dormant. This can cause the board to exist in a kind of perpetual atrophy, where meetings turn into nothing more than motion-seconding marathons. Because there is so much potential energy waiting to explode, passionate board members often make the unintentional mistake of finding improper outlets for their energies.

A board's Program Committee, for example, may begin to take over an organization's programming, even when there is a paid Program Director on staff. Suddenly talented board members find that their energies are being channeled in the wrong directions. A woman with a brilliant knack for fundraising ends up choosing the tablecloth colors for a special event; a man with an uncanny gift for strategizing winds up in charge of mailings. When this happens, people become quickly dissatisfied. No one signed on to be a lump on a log or an envelope-licker. That's not what it means to be a member of a thriving, exciting, empowering board.

The Bigger Picture

Nonprofit boards that can use the above adjectives to describe themselves generally have one thing in common: they've got their eyes on the bigger picture.

And "bigger picture" doesn't just mean fundraising. Many people assume that a board's preeminent prerogative is fundraising, especially since there's a sort of anxiety attached to fundraising for most nonprofits. Fundraising is important, but it actually shouldn't come first. Here's a circular graph illustrating the dilemma of knowing where to begin. Which activity do *you* think ought to take priority over the rest?

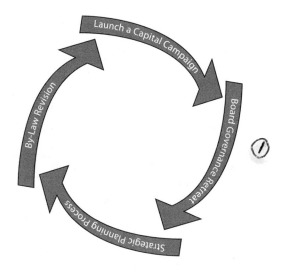

I highly recommend that you schedule a board governance retreat as your first move. It's essential that both board and CEO have a good grasp of your governance model before moving on to anything else. Once you've done that, you've paved the way for more meaningful strategic planning. Then you can turn your attention to issues like fundraising. On the Board Engagement Matrix, you'll notice that budgeting and finance are included in the tactical category, which is midway down the diagram. These issues are very important, but need to be framed by the primary and fundamental issues. In other words, you have to know who you are before you decide what kind of plans you're going to make to get there.

YOU HAVE TO KNOW YOUR ROLE BEFORE YOU KNOW YOUR GOAL

Imagine that an all-around. top-notch athlete is tapped to try out for the 2012 Olympics. They tell her, "You're going to have to train forty hours a week, tighten your leg muscles, work on building arm strength, and lose ten pounds, but we think you've got the potential. Now let's get started." How do you think that athlete's going to respond? The first thing she says will probably be something along the lines of, "Um, what sport am I going for?" Before she embarks on an intensive training program, she needs to know in which sport she'll be expected to compete. It's pretty important that she knows whether she'll be a gymnast or a swimmer!

Nonprofits work exactly the same way. An organization's system of governance must be clearly understood before the board and CEO embark on a capital campaign or strategy. In other words, you can't start drawing up your strategic plan until you know exactly what your role is as a governor.

Navigating the governance-management line at the heart of Principle I is a continual source of struggle for many nonprofits. The CEO of an agency promoting childhood literacy, a woman who had formerly served as a member of several nonprofit boards, put it like this: "It's very hard for a board member to know what they're supposed to do. It's just something that's never been answered for me in the past as a board member. Where do my responsibilities end and the staff's begin? When you don't have any boundaries, they're set by each individual board member. Some want very little to do with the operations, and some want way more than they should."

After I worked closely with this agency to establish clear expectations and roles, the CEO noted a marked improvement in the way the organization did business. When hiring decisions came up and the board wanted to vet potential staff members, she was able to put the brakes on and say, "I appreciate your commitment to this organization and will be sure to ask for your input when needed. I'll provide you with a report on our hires, but let's make sure we're on the same page as to who's making the ultimate hiring decision." As a gentle reminder, she emailed the Six Principles to the board and emphasized the first principle. She and the board members were able to agree that hiring was a management, not a governance, issue. "It gave us guidelines rather than a power struggle," she said. "Now we know how to handle an individual situation."

Governance vs. Management

One subset of the nonprofit world that is particularly susceptible to confusing governance with management is the private and independent school realm. Because most schools typically have a high percentage of parents sitting on the board of trustees, personal interests and passions can easily creep into the fray, often unintentionally. I once received a newsletter from a private school announcing that, after a long and spirited discussion, the board had decided to rescind the one-dollar tardy policy. You can guess what was wrong with that picture: it's not something that should constitute a long and drawn-out board meeting. Not that it isn't an important issue—for parents and children, a dollar is a dollar, and tardiness is a veritable concern. But this is a staff issue, not something that should keep the board up at night.

Parents serving as trustees aren't the only ones who have a vested interest in the nonprofits they serve. In fact many nonprofit board members are either direct consumers of the organization's services, or they have been at some point in the past. This is one of the biggest boons in a nonprofit's favor: passionate, well-intentioned board members who are intimately connected to the organization and believe wholeheartedly in its mission. But personal concerns can easily spill over and muddy the board's priorities. A board member at an organization for heart disease, for example, may have a problem with a specific staff member who's taken over a program he once participated in; perhaps he dislikes the way the new person is handling things. Because of these kinds of conflicts, I typically suggest that no more than 50 percent of the board be made up of direct consumers.

The CEO of an Oklahoma nonprofit gave his own take on how the distinction between governance and management plays out. "I would say 90 percent of CEO turnover is related to violations of the first principle. If you're not talking about things from a fifty-thousand-foot level—like what you're going to do to anticipate a demographic shift in the community—and instead you're talking about fights among the office staff, you're doing a major disservice. With so many direct consumers also serving as board members, they've got to understand that they're not there to manage the programs or make personnel decisions. They're there to make sure they are stewarding the organization so that the next generation of community members will have the opportunity to take advantage." That kind of long-term thinking is precisely what governance is all about.

RECRUITING NONPARENTS TO YOUR SCHOOL BOARD

Many people in the private school world ask, "How do you get a nonparent to serve on the board?" The answer I give is that when a person's qualities and abilities are being used to the hilt, they will be most happy to engage in a mission they believe in. This opens the board up to allow for fresh and useful perspectives.

Alternately, disengaged boards do their organizations a great disservice. I once visited a small university where the president had been there for thirty years. This kind of longevity was great for him, but the students and the faculty were suffering. There was little board oversight and zero accountability. The main push was to enroll moneyed students, even ones who didn't meet the standards of the institution, solely to fill their coffers and attract wealthy parents to the board.

Founder's Syndrome

Then there's the problem of Founder's Syndrome, an issue that plagues a number of nonprofit organizations. Founder's Syndrome occurs when board members start out as founders of the nonprofit. Since many organizations aren't able to hire professionals in their early stages, the board's incipient role includes creating handbooks, dealing with publicity issues, and handling other management duties. Once the organization *is* able to hire a CEO and staff, the board has trouble breaking out of their initial role and letting go. A board that falls victim to Founder's Syndrome often finds itself unable to delegate to the professional; as a result, the CEO is unable to do his or her job.

In actuality, I would argue that the founding board is not really a board. Of course legally you are, but you're not truly a board until you hire a CEO, empower him or her to hire a professional staff, and let all of them do their jobs.

Many people working in nonprofits assign a lot of weight to syndromes and cycles, timelines and evolutions, and all of the technical labels slapped on a board in an effort to identify and "fix" the problem. Under the Six Principles model, these cycles ultimately don't matter—it's an indefatigable system that is applicable to all boards. This doesn't mean that boards can adopt all six principles at once; it's a process, and like any process, it takes time. But in order to be a true governing board, a board must agree to take action, adopt a set of principles, and move forward on them. According to this model, it all starts with a conscious decision to choose governance over management, letting the professional staff attend to its issues while the board members focus on the bigger picture.

THE CONSENT AGENDA

A useful tool for helping boards focus on governance is a consent agenda. A consent agenda gets all of the housekeeping and other minutiae out of the way before each meeting begins. Issues put under a consent agenda don't need any discussion before a vote. If a board member requests that an item be removed from the agenda so that it can be discussed, that item is taken off and the rest of the consent agenda is voted on without any further discussion.

Typical items that go on a consent agenda are routine and standard issues such as office reports, going over previous meeting minutes, minor procedural changes, updating documents, and confirming traditional contracts. Items which would not be appropriate for a consent agenda are topics that deal with strategy, major policy revisions, mission, or anything else that falls near the top of the Board Engagement Matrix.

When used correctly, the consent agenda can free up significant chunks of meeting time so that the board can focus on other things—like going over a governance model and discussing how to adopt the principles it proposes.

Focusing on Mission

Tantamount to focusing on the bigger picture is deciding on the organization's mission. Why does your nonprofit exist? Whom does it serve, and how does it provide a service? This is where the line becomes easily blurred—if a board diverts its attention to the ways in which it is providing a service, it runs the risk of edging into the terrain of management. If board members spend their time collecting box tops and choosing invitation templates, for example, how are they going to move the organization where it needs to be ten years from now? Often people who really want to see tangible, immediate change in an organization they care about would perform better and feel more fulfilled as volunteers than they would as board members. A board's role is thoughtful, patient, and conducive to long-term change and improvement. A nonprofit's mission should be created with the big picture in mind.

Most organizations must make significant decisions in regard to their mission. Is a nonprofit going to serve only children, or both children and their families? Is a school going to be single sex or co-ed? Will a museum expand beyond merely hosting exhibits to serve as an educational center in the community? Sometimes mission questions are geographical in nature—is an organization's service area in just one county, or will it include neighboring areas? At the heart of the mission is the question: whom are we to serve? Once these key questions are answered, a board can look at ways to preserve and perpetuate the mission while looking forward.

Twenty-five Seconds in the Elevator

In my work with nonprofit boards, I often suggest that they create a twenty-five-second "elevator speech," a simple pitch outlining the central purpose of their organization that they can share if they were to bump into an interested party in an elevator. The more practical application of this piece is that it can be used to solicit donations, but theoretically it can help board members get a sense of their purpose and responsibilities as governors. A twenty-five-second speech is something all members can memorize and take to heart, and it helps to clarify their mission and strategies. For example, a twenty-five-second elevator speech for a museum I worked with had five parts:

1. A one-sentence summary of the museum's purpose and importance.
2. Brief summaries of three of the museum's primary activities.
3. A description of the special need for citywide awareness and education.
4. The fact that the museum is the only center bearing this agenda in the surrounding area; no other organization exists to meet this need.
5. An invitation to share in this effort, for what it would mean to both the city and the donor.

Revisiting the Governance Model

Like any governance model, the Six Principles require time and commitment. Typically, the organizations that experience the most success are the ones that continue to revisit the Six Principles model and measure their progress. (In fact, one of my clients chose to place the Six Principles on the back of their board members' tent card.) A CEO at one nonprofit told me that she found it extremely helpful to keep things before board members so that they could continue to build on what they'd learned. After undergoing a significant shift in board makeup and deciding to adopt the Six Principles model, her organization continued to go back and revisit it, paying especially close attention to the

Board Engagement Matrix. When several members of the new board thought they were going to be responsible for administrative decisions, the Matrix was brought out and shared, the main thrust of the conversation being: these are the things the board focuses on, and these are the things the administration focuses on. "That tool was so helpful in relieving anxieties," a board member said. "People thought that the board had to make all the decisions." But with a clear idea of their duties and responsibilities, they were able to forge ahead and focus on the real work of a thriving, governing board.

Remember Teresa Thompson, the dedicated yet conflicted board member from our story? After the fiasco with the invitations stirred up so much controversy amongst the Life with Leukemia board, Teresa felt responsible for dragging the organization into confusion and, wracked with guilt, was seriously contemplating turning in her resignation. Sherri, the CEO of Life with Leukemia, realized she was at risk of losing one of their strongest supporters and most vibrant board members. Around the same time, Sherri heard about a conference devoted entirely to nonprofit governance being held in the area. She decided to attend.

As it so happened, the conference featured the Six Principles model. While sitting in the audience, Sherri found herself increasingly excited as the workshop continued. She approached me after my presentation and described her situation. "If I can get the board to sign on," she told me, "I think this could really change the way we do things." She also knew exactly how she was going to whet the board's appetite: the Board Engagement Matrix.

At the next board meeting, Sherri brought copies of the Matrix and circulated them to all the board members. They discussed Principle I in depth, and how the board's job was to focus on governance, not management. As a result of the discussion, the members of the Planning Committee relinquished control of the invitation decision, which was then delegated to two staff members. Within the week, the staff members had come up with a beautiful design that both parties were pleased with.

After passing out the Matrix in the October board meeting, Sherri shared with the board what she'd learned from the Six Principles model. She said she thought it would be extremely fruitful to introduce the system to the rest of the board. A lot of board members were unsure. "We'll think about it," was the general response. "At some point in the future, maybe."

But for Teresa Thompson, the immediate results were positive. She walked out of the October meeting with the Matrix firmly in hand, feeling relieved and happy to be a governing member of an organization she believed in.

Life with Leukemia's journey had just begun.

Principle II

The Board Has One Employee: the CEO

Mid-November

A Board Member Oversteps His Boundaries

After spending the last twenty-five years as a CPA, Allan Jameson knows a thing or two about numbers. He's an extremely astute and analytical thinker; he's also a very capable business manager. Years ago he started his own accounting firm which quickly grew to be one of the most successful firms in the district, and he recently retired very comfortably. When he lost his mother to leukemia last year, Allan became very active in the cancer community and donated a large sum of money to help fund cancer research. Because he's such a shrewd businessman, Life with Leukemia took notice. The board asked him to serve as a board member, and Allan accepted, eager to make his mark and contribute his expertise.

No one at Life with Leukemia doubts Allan's expertise—his personal track record is a testament to his financial acumen and business savvy. He's certainly got more experience in accounting than any of the other board members. Everyone's been well aware of this from the beginning. But the problem is that Allan is aware of it too. Suddenly without a business to run and with a good deal of extra time on his hands, he's decided to take it upon himself to bring the accounting aspects of the business up to par. Allan's reasoning follows this train of thought: "If Life with Leukemia is going to be a world-class organization, then we've got to completely revolutionize the way we do our books." A naturally competitive businessman and a visionary thinker, Allan envisions substantial growth for Life with Leukemia—ten years down the line, he sees it as the next American Cancer Society, and as such he wants to ensure that it runs like a well-oiled machine. In his mind, fully functional finances are paramount to an organization's success.

So, Allan starts to cultivate a relationship with Jerry, the Life with Leukemia finance director. Jerry just got his MBA and only has three years of experience, but he's exceptionally bright and eager to learn. When Allan starts dropping by the office, Jerry is always happy to see him; the distinguished CPA is something of a celebrity in the community, and the young finance director figures he can learn a lot from him. But when Allan starts making suggestions as to how the books should be kept—he thinks Life with Leukemia should invest in an advanced new software package called ChecksMate instead of the standard QuickBooks they've been using—Jerry gets a little worried. While he originally considered this man as a kind of mentor, he now finds himself in the awkward position of taking advice from a board member, instead of answering directly to his superior, the Life with Leukemia CEO.

When Jerry finally drums up the courage to express his discomfort, Allan feels affronted. What started as a friendship between them quickly turns into an unpleasant and caustic connection. In Allan's mind, Jerry is to blame. Not only is he unqualified for the position, but he's intentionally blocking all of Allan's well-intentioned attempts to encourage growth and progress in the organization. After all, Allan was only trying to use his ample experience to better Life with Leukemia and make it a stronger nonprofit. Isn't that what he joined the board to do? Everyone on the board knew this was his area of expertise; it follows that they must want his input. Just who does this Jerry character think he is?

At the November board meeting, Allan makes a suggestion. He states his claim that, drawing on many years of personal experience in the field, he thinks that Life with Leukemia should adopt some new principles and restrictions to tighten up their bookkeeping. They should begin using ChecksMate, restructure the budget, and most importantly, only hire staff in the finance department with at least five years of accounting experience. Some members of the board are thrilled by Allan's suggestion; it seems apparent to them that with his help, the organization could really reach to a whole new level. But other members—Teresa Thompson among them—are suspicious of Allan's motives. Does this audacious proposal have anything to do with his dislike of Jerry, perhaps?

Though he may think he's doing a service to Life with Leukemia, Allan is acting in direct violation of Principle II of the Six Principles: The board has one employee and one employee alone: the CEO.

The Board Member's Role

A basic tenet of governance is that the board hires the CEO who in turn hires all the other staff. The board views the CEO's role as similar to that of a Chief Executive in the corporate world; thus, all accountability rests upon the CEO alone. No one staff member is accountable to the board and certainly not to any individual board member.

The moment Allan began to bypass the CEO and communicate directly with the finance director, he was breaking the chain of communication and treating Jerry as an employee. If Allan had a legitimate concern about the accounting software being used, or even if he had specific worries about Jerry's performance, the correct course of action would have been to approach the CEO directly and talk it over with her. Allan wasn't just being meddlesome. He ran the risk of undermining the authority of the CEO and in so doing, harming the dynamics of the board.

It's a gray area, to be sure. These things are very rarely black and white. A situation will surely arise when there *is* a legitimate reason to be concerned with the performance of a certain staff member. In this scenario, every well-intentioned board member may wonder, "How can I *not* say something? I care about this organization too much to stay silent!" The problem comes when the board member decides to approach the staff member directly, instead of honoring the process and expressing his or her concerns to the CEO instead.

Nonprofit board members typically hail from many different fields, and many of them are experts in their own right. A hospital board may include retired physicians and medical experts; school boards will include parents, former professors, and even heads of school culled from other institutions; a foundation might glean some outstanding members of the community for its coveted board seats. Most boards feature a dizzying array of advanced degrees, business credentials, and social networking prowess. Each individual contributes his or her own specialized knowledge, and when combined, the board as a whole benefits from many years of sage wisdom and practical know-how covering a broad spectrum of interests. This is one of the most advantageous assets of a nonprofit board.

The downside is that despite their breadth of knowledge and expertise, board members often don't have enough clarity about their exact roles as members of the board. And, like Allan Jameson, they want to contribute to the organization in the ways they know best. The finances of Life with Leukemia were not under Allan's jurisdiction, but because he had the right background and qualifications, Allan didn't see how he was overstepping his boundaries. When a process for addressing concerns with the CEO and the CEO alone hasn't been established, there are no checks and balances in place. Most board members are genuinely passionate and interested in bettering the organization they serve; the problem is that no one's taken the time to delineate what their job entails and what it doesn't.

Of course, there are always some situations where board members intentionally go behind the back of the CEO. At one midsize organization created to conserve the rich heritage of a local community, the board member who handled facility maintenance stopped speaking to the CEO after an extended argument. After their falling out, the board member would only communicate through one of the staff members—he would never speak directly to the CEO about anything. But generally speaking, most board members aren't trying to be vindictive. They're simply unclear as to what role they're supposed to play.

Many board members struggle with the basic precept behind Principle II. When you have a legitimate interest in your organization, the natural impulse is to reach in and fix things that seem to be going wrong. A lot of board members are real go-getters who champion a do-it-yourself attitude; if they have a problem or concern, they prefer to go directly to a staff member instead of bothering the CEO—especially if he or she is busy or inaccessible. But time and again, well-intentioned members of an organization unwittingly chip away at the board/CEO partnership when they fail to acknowledge the CEO as the one employee of the board. When the board begins overly interacting with the staff, what kind of power does the CEO have over his or her own staff? Not much. If Allan were to successfully pass his motion that staff members in finance have a minimum of five years' accounting experience, who's really doing the hiring and firing for Life with Leukemia? It certainly isn't the CEO. It's the board, or in this case, one well-intentioned businessman who sits on it.

Volunteers as Board Members

In my work with nonprofits, I've found that Principle II is most commonly endangered when a former volunteer joins the board as a trustee. Because volunteers have had an active hand in the management duties of the organization, they often don't understand that management is under the CEO's jurisdiction. A few years ago, I was working closely with a large nonprofit in the health sector when they experienced a caustic blowup. After being elected to the board, a hardworking volunteer began serving on the technology committee. He was hell-bent on keeping spending down, and before long he was requesting receipts from Best Buy and expressing his myriad worries directly to the staff.

Fresh from the Six Principles workshop, the CEO recognized the problem quickly and knew she had to nip it in the bud. She contacted him on a Friday, asking that he limit his interaction with her team and forward his comments and questions through her until an understanding could be reached about governance versus management. She also informed him that she had asked for copies of emails from staff where he had expressed concerns or questions.

On Sunday, two days after hearing from the CEO, the volunteer/board member sent out an email to all of the organization's volunteers. In his email, he said that he was "embarrassed that [his] enthusiasm regarding fundraising for technology improvement had been used against [him]." He questioned the CEO's credibility and, in response to her request for copies of emails from staff, he requested specific examples of times when volunteers felt they had been misled, ignored, or even lied to. "Please be as specific as possible," he urged. "I hope this will lead to a better understanding of the relationship of volunteers to our organization." He signed the email with his name and the tagline, "Writing only for myself as a volunteer."

THE BOARD MEMBER'S HAT

At least in perception, a board member never ceases to be a board member—they are always wearing their board member "hats." When board members speak to staff in an advisory capacity, it puts staff members in an uncomfortable position. And because an organization's staff members are generally eager to do good work, it's difficult for them to take what a board member suggests with a grain of salt.

Now this isn't to say that a board member can't have a conversation with a staff member. In most nonprofits, these types of interactions are frequent; avoiding them would be senseless if not impossible. It simply means that board members must be ever cognizant of the fact that when they speak to a member of the staff, they are always wearing a conspicuous board hat. Even if Allan had approached Jerry and said, "You know, Jerry, I'm not coming to you as a board member. I just want to share some ideas with you that you can think over," Jerry would still view him as a member of the Life with Leukemia board.

Because of this, trustees must make an active choice to weigh their words carefully in every conversation with a staff member.

Volunteer or not, he was also a board member, and as such his actions were extremely out of line. In and of themselves, his concerns were reasonable—what nonprofit can't save some money here and there? But despite the fact that the nonprofit was on budget and meeting its goals, his grievances continued to fester until they reared their head in a most disruptive way. The moment the board began spending valuable meeting time unpacking Best Buy receipts, it created an environment of bad karma and disengagement. Yet no board member stood up against him when he started to pull them off track.

The incendiary email was the final straw. At that point he was using his position as a board member to exert inappropriate leverage on the volunteers—without whom the organization would surely crumble—not to mention using his prestige to enact a personal vendetta against the CEO. After his email circulated up the ranks, the CEO and board chair concluded that they would have to ask the member to step down. The board chair informed him that he could no longer serve on the board, and the nonprofit worked hard to ameliorate the damage caused by his negative influence.

The Nonprofit Executive as CEO

Though the corporate world is rife with its own set of problems, this is one area in which they typically have fewer troubles than nonprofits. For one thing, most corporate board members get paid to sit on boards; sometimes their compensation is more than most people's yearly salary. Since nonprofit board members are essentially volunteering their time and efforts, and the CEO is a paid professional, an awkward dynamic can arise between the two branches. But CEOs have to understand that they need to lead up. In a corporate environment, it's pretty well understood that when you hire a CEO, the buck stops at that individual. Accountability rests solely with the CEO, who generally feels a real sense of ownership. As a result, the company looks to that figure and that figure alone. Of course attaching so much weight to one individual has its drawbacks—a corrupt CEO, for example, can topple an entire corporate entity because when he or she goes down, the reputation of the whole company is extirpated.

There are all kinds of issues from Corporate America that we don't want to bring into our nonprofit world—on the whole, nonprofits embrace a more holistic world view, dedicating real passion and commitment to the issues and serving the community. But there still needs to be some sense of hierarchy in an organization, and there has to be somebody who makes the final decision. It can be a very positive thing if the CEO of a nonprofit bears the same responsibilities as a CEO at a company in the public or private sector. You can still run your nonprofit and dream your dreams with as much idealism as you need—as long as you have someone who is accountable.

After I led a retreat for a nonprofit that worked with youth in the community, the CEO noted how important Principle II was to her organization. Before they adopted the Six Principles model, there was one board member who had been going directly to a staff person, getting information and assigning tasks for that person to do, and was edging dangerously close to doing the work herself. After the retreat, the CEO was able to tactfully remind the board member of the chain of communication. And after the board and the CEO discussed *why* they all benefited from having that system in place and the dangers that arose from not abiding by it, the board member was happy to oblige. "It's really important to have that framework," the CEO said. "That way it doesn't become your judgment versus their judgment. Instead it's 'this is the way we want to behave as an organization.'"

The CEO at another nonprofit offered equally positive feedback after implementing Principle II. After my work with the organization, all parties involved emerged with a clear understanding of the fact that the board had only one employee: the CEO. The staff and administrators were directly responsible only to him. As he put it, before adopting the Six Principles they "had people who were violating that boundary—not in a malicious way, but because they were familiar with some people on the staff. It's confusing when board members have conversations with senior staff members that get into the day-to-day-business; it makes people very uncomfortable. Ultimately, we as CEOs are accountable."

Sherri Steps Up as CEO

So what happened at Life with Leukemia? Armed with a copy of the Six Principles, Sherri approached Allan Jameson privately about the situation. This led to a very candid discussion regarding Allan's interaction with Jerry. At first Allan couldn't see how he'd done anything wrong, but the more they talked about it, the more he began to see how his behavior was out of bounds. He's still concerned about the organization's bookkeeping not being up to snuff, so he and Sherri have scheduled a time with Jerry to discuss the pros and cons of updating their accounting software. In the meantime, he rescinded his motion for a five-year minimal experience requirement. Jerry kept his job and received no further surprise office visits from the legendary CPA.

Principle III

The CEO Has Only One Employer: the Board as a Whole

December

Trouble for the CEO

Ever since she was little, Sherri Talbot, the CEO of Life with Leukemia, has felt called to make a difference in the world. She grew up in a small town and started volunteering at the local hospital as a teenager. During her days working with cancer patients, she befriended Carly Snowdon, a girl who came frequently to the hospital to visit her uncle. Soon, Carly and Sherri were like sisters;

they developed a fast friendship that would remain strong for the next twenty years. They wound up going to the same university, both majoring in business, and when they started their families, they brought the whole gang together for barbecues and cookouts on holidays and weekends. Even their kids were best of friends.

As a prominent businesswoman in the community, Carly had been serving on the board of Life with Leukemia for some time when the previous CEO retired. As soon as the board began screening applicants for the newly opened position, she suggested Sherri for the job. Sherri couldn't have been happier with the opportunity—she was tired of working in the corporate world and leapt at the chance to lead an organization she loved that provided a service she believed in. The whole board was impressed by Sherri's qualifications and her legitimate commitment to the organization's mission. She was hired on the spot.

The first two years of Sherri's tenure as CEO went very smoothly. She was competent and skilled, a passionate leader with a real vision for the future. But when Sherri started struggling with issues in her personal life, they began to spill over into her professional performance, especially in the wake of a difficult divorce.

As a result, she's been asleep at the wheel when it comes to her executive responsibilities at Life with Leukemia. The organization's services are in disarray, and the staff doesn't feel very focused. Sherri promised to speak with Allan Jameson about updating their bookkeeping software, but she keeps canceling appointments. Her original passion for implementing the Six Principles model has taken a backseat to everything else going on in her life. The board is a little worried about her, and Carly is more worried than anyone. She hates to see her best friend struggling through such a hard time. Carly, who was formerly serving as the Life with Leukemia vice chair, has also just been appointed as the new chairwoman of the board.

Twenty minutes before the last board meeting of the year, Carly pulls Sherri aside. It's obvious that she's upset and stressed—several board members have been complaining, and she's worried about losing her job on top of everything else. Carly decides to put her mind at ease. "I know there've been some issues with various board members," she says, "but listen, Sher, for the next two years while I am chair, you're safe. You have my word that no one's going to touch you. I know you and the kids are suffering, and I don't want you to have to worry about things at work on top of everything else. I promise that your position as CEO is secure. After all, it's really the least I can do." Sherri smiles gratefully, and the meeting begins.

What just happened? It could be argued that Carly is a true friend, supporting Sherri through a trying time. But as the recently elected board chair of Life with Leukemia, Carly isn't just Sherri's buddy—she's a governor of an organization. By making her best friend that kind of promise, she just overstepped a huge boundary by defying Principle III of the Six Principles: the CEO has only one employer, the board as a whole.

The third principle is deceptively simple. It may seem obvious that the CEO serves the board as a whole instead of its individual members. But when we move beyond conceptual relevance into the realm of practical application, the waters get a little murkier. Situations like the exchange between Sherri and Carly are not uncommon occurrences among many nonprofits. Again, it's a boundary issue, and so often the boundaries aren't clearly defined for board members or CEOs.

When we talk about governance, we're not talking about protecting someone's tenure. Governance is about protecting the mission and the people an organization serves. A board that ethically governs makes it known that the CEO is responsible only to the unified board. The moment Carly assured Sherri that she wouldn't lose her job, she was no longer accountable to the board as a unified entity but to a single person—in this case her close friend and chair of the board. Though Carly was trying to do Sherri a favor in this particular scenario, sometimes the CEO is beholden to a board member in more negative and subversive ways. By adhering to Principle III, an organization can avoid political pressure on the CEO to field the special interests of individual trustees. In a healthy organization, board members understand that their collective responsibility takes precedence over their individual relationships with the CEO.

How Many Bosses Do You Have?

When I get to Principle III in my seminars, I pose two questions to the CEOs in the room. "How many board members do you have?" is my first question. The answer varies—sometimes it's a number like fifteen or twenty; sometimes it's more in the range of seven to nine, depending on the size of the organization. It's when I ask the next question—"How many bosses do you have?"—that things *really* get interesting.

Sometimes "one" is the response I get. But sometimes the answer is a long way from one. A lot of times the same number pops up as the answer to both questions—for example, a CEO will say that he has fifteen board members and thus fifteen bosses. The executive committee and the board chair often exert their own distinct voices, and sometimes each individual is positing his or her own ideas. The answer to the second question should, of course, be one. And that "one" is not the board chair. As we discussed at the outset of this chapter, if all is functioning as it ought to in a nonprofit, the CEO has one boss: the board as a single unit. And a unified board doesn't mean you have to dance around the table at board meetings, holding hands and singing "Kumbaya." It simply means that each member of the board gets one equal vote, and only one. After they've cast that vote, they act as one body, and any lingering disagreements or individual concerns must be set aside for the good of the whole board. For a number of nonprofits, this means changing the whole paradigm they've been using for years.

At many organizations, there's a kind of unspoken understanding that the board chair, or other powerful board member, gets more than one vote. Though it's never verbalized, this latent belief can still have an incredibly detrimental effect on an organization. The Six Principles model reframes the role of the chair because so often, CEOs live and die by the chair. I firmly believe that it's capricious to have a system where every one or two years, when a new chair is appointed, a whole new cycle begins, bringing with it a different set of expectations. Suddenly an organization is relegated to operating under the chair du jour, which often translates into the whim du jour—not very conducive to long-term vision or planning.

The way to avoid this kind of upheaval is to always be wary of assigning a disproportionate amount of power to the board chair. The chairman's role is undeniably important, but instead of spearheading the board, the role should be one of cooperative facilitation. It is the chair's job to facilitate a strong relationship between the collective board and the CEO. After all, it's not the *chair/CEO* partnership that concerns us; it's the Six Principles of *Board*/CEO Partnerships.

In traditional models of nonprofit governance, the chair is often pitted as the bad cop. It doesn't have to be this way. Many people assert that a person who is inherently nonconfrontational may have a hard time being an effective board chair. This outlook poses a problem when you consider that amicable board members with good people skills are often appointed to the position of chair. Who wouldn't want a board chair who can act as a positive cheerleader and consensus-builder for the organization? That's especially true when a nonprofit is still smarting from the previous tenure of a particularly divisive, rigid chairman. But what happens, people wonder fearfully, if the new chair is unable to reel in renegade board members who overstep their boundaries?

When a nonprofit chooses to adopt the Six Principles model, an easy solution presents itself: *any* board member is empowered to confront a vigilante colleague, purely by definition of being a board member. Everyone has one vote, remember? So if a fellow board member is out of line and the board chairman doesn't step up to the plate to fortify the board/CEO partnership (or pass out copies of the Board Engagement Matrix), the other members of the board are equally qualified to speak up about the situation. Instead of always deferring to the chair, the whole board is responsible for the behavior of its individual members. As we will see in the next chapter, members of the governance committee can consciously fulfill this purpose.

No one member should be privileged above any other—not the board chair, not the head of a powerful committee, really no one at all. There aren't any exceptions. For an organization to truly embrace Principle III, everyone must be in agreement that *all* board members are created equal. The CEO should neither depend too heavily on one person—like Sherri depending on Carly—or be cowed by the influence of any individual member. This protects the board, the CEO, and most importantly, the beneficiaries of the organization itself, paving the way for the nonprofit to build a stronger governance culture.

The Problem with Special Privileges

There's a very potent example I like to use to illustrate Principle III. I've changed the names, but the story is true. Mr. Jones was a powerful member of the board at an elite private school. His daughter Linda was about to enter the eighth grade when Mr. Jones heard through the grapevine that the school was making a switch. They were bringing in a new eighth grade teacher, a young and idealistic transplant from the East Coast. Shortly after he heard the news, Mr. Jones stopped the head of the school in the hallway and said very congenially, "I heard you're bringing in a new teacher to the eighth grade."

"Oh, yes," said the head. "Mrs. Samson is retiring this year, and we're bringing in this terrific candidate from Dartmouth. We're very excited about it."

Mr. Jones was silent for a moment. When he spoke, he was dangerously quiet. "Do you think having a first-year teacher is really a good thing for the school community?"

"Absolutely," the head answered. "She has a great curriculum planned for next year." And that was it. The conversation was over . . . at least for the head, who assumed that to be the end of the discussion.

Unfortunately, it wasn't. At the next board meeting a few days later, Mr. Jones made an unexpected motion. Much like Allan Jameson at Life with Leukemia, he suddenly wanted to create a restriction on staff hiring, seemingly out of the blue. "We're a community school, and the eighth grade is our top class," he said to the board. "I strongly feel that the teachers of the eighth grade should have an advanced degree."

The head of school's jaw practically dropped to the floor. But the motion passed—despite the fact that it wasn't on the agenda—and three months later, the head was no longer with the school because everyone on the faculty knew it wasn't the head who decided who was teaching. It was the board or maybe even Mr. Jones himself.

I've witnessed endless variations on the same theme. Say a board member makes a phone call to the CEO to mention that a friend or child is looking for a job or internship. If that happens, it's the CEO's responsibility to say, "Thanks—I appreciate the heads up. But so-and-so will need to apply through the regular process. That way we can make sure to do this in the most transparent way." If the conversation ends there, great. But if the board member continues to needle the CEO, he or she is guilty of exerting inappropriate force over hiring and firing concerns, which fall firmly under the executive's control. If the CEO caves, then a culture of nepotism and unfair advantage has been established—not a good precedent to be set.

At one nonprofit, a situation arose when the CEO of a museum made plans to let go of a veteran curator who had been on staff for nearly thirty years. The quality of the curator's tours was floundering, and it was clear that visitors to the museum were no longer benefiting from her curatorship. This woman knew she was under the gun, so when she got wind of the CEO's intentions, she did all she could to hold on for dear life. What was her first course of action? She called up the wife of a board member, who happened to be her friend and Wednesday night bridge partner, and said, "They can't do this to me." You can imagine what happened: she guaranteed her own protection, and six months later, the CEO, stripped of any real power, left the museum. The curator got to keep her cushy job. Who ends up suffering in this scenario? The people who should be benefiting from the museum's services, of course.

Giving Your CEO the Opportunity to Fail

Principle III lays down the law: it is never a board member's place to guarantee immunity to anyone, whether it's a staff member, faculty member, or the CEO herself. At the other extreme, it is also utterly unacceptable for a board member to co-opt the board in an effort to overthrow an executive. In my observations, this latter scenario is most often what occurs.

I once witnessed a stunning example of this at a midsize nonprofit in the environmental sector. Leading this organization was a woman we'll call Cecilia. Cecilia was a very capable CEO and a superb fundraiser, but she didn't exactly have the best people skills. To put it bluntly, she was a bull in a china shop. Cecilia could be brusque and unpleasant, and as a result, many members of the board of directors found her personality off-putting. One particularly disgruntled board member, Monica, was eager to clean house; she saw getting rid of Cecilia as the perfect opportunity to wipe the slate clean and start fresh.

In the hopes of reestablishing their focus and recommitting themselves to their mission, the board planned a mission retreat. But Monica hijacked the retreat on day one before the work had even begun. In a board of twenty, she stood up and said, "You know what? I know we're here to talk about mission and all that, but we're not going anywhere with Cecilia at the helm. I want to request an executive session of the board." Just like that, they threw Cecilia out of the room, and she sat outside waiting for the inevitable.

After three long hours, the board reemerged. "We'll have a meeting tomorrow," they said, but it was already apparent what would happen. Sure enough, Cecilia was unceremoniously fired the next day.

Some time later, one of the board members said to me by way of explanation, "You know, Jonathan, it's never a good time to grow a beard. But sometimes you have to grow one." This roughly translates to: "It's never a good time to throw out your CEO, but sometimes you have to do it." It didn't matter that this particular CEO was about to procure a $200,000 gift for the organization; because her personality rubbed people the wrong way and one outspoken board member couldn't take it anymore, she was cast off without so much as an explanation. They lost the gift, of course. Not to mention a competent leader who, if she had been given the chance to iron out the kinks in her personality, might have taken the organization to a whole new level of success.

Many organizations manage to avoid either extreme. Plenty of nonprofits are fortunate enough to never suffer under a Carly/Sherri-type agreement or a Monica vs. Cecilia battle. But even if unresolved tensions never come to a head, any CEO who feels she is working for multiple bosses should confront the issue. It's a dangerous position for the board, and it's a dangerous position for the CEO. The bottom line is that people are successful when they know to whom and for what they're responsible. Let's not even worry about giving people the opportunity to succeed; we should at least give them the opportunity to fail.

Some years after the Cecilia incident, I observed a similar situation arise with a CEO, but this story had quite a different ending. Martin was the CEO of the local chapter of an arts nonprofit and, like Cecilia, he struggled with limited people skills, yet he brought an extensive arts background to the table. The board was at a standstill; half the board wanted Martin out while the other half supported him. The national organization overseeing the nonprofit brought me in to try and broker the situation, and in our work together, I encouraged the board to give Martin the opportunity to fail. So the board called a meeting and agreed to give him some time with a professional coach to see if things changed. In six months, a committee would reevaluate his progress with the board.

Six months later, Martin's people skills had shown a marked improvement. He was still no Casanova, but he was able to keep his position as CEO, which he held for the next three years until it was time for him to move on. When he did, the board threw a party to express their gratitude that he had provided what they needed at the time they needed it. Of course, if Martin had shown no improvement, the board would have been justified in letting him go and seeking someone who meshed better with the organization. The point is: this board gave Martin the opportunity to fail. And like many CEOs, when given that opportunity, Martin found a way to succeed.

Constructing a One-Boss System

It is completely unethical to work for more than one boss. No one can function while working with twenty different special interests. This breeds a lack of certainty and stability, which can be lethal to a nonprofit; it doesn't take much for a CEO to start feeling overwhelmed by trying to please everyone. Now, I don't mean to imply that each board member should not be treated as an individual. I encourage CEOs to go out to lunch with each board member on occasion—everyone wants their opinions to be heard. It's a great idea for CEOs to get to know each of their board members, to discover their unique interests and values and passions. But setting up deals with individual board members is never a good idea, and CEOs should avoid anything that makes them feel a need to placate twenty different people. You can argue it's all about politics, politics, politics, but it doesn't have to be that way. The Six Principles model ensures that it won't be.

The CEO of an international agency reflected on the differences in how the organization operated before and after choosing to implement the Six Principles: "We had a prior chairman who ran the thing a little too much like a fiefdom, but when we adopted the new model, it encouraged all board members to realize they have an ownership and also that I work for the board. The board now knows that I hire and fire, and very rarely does any director go around me. We changed our bylaws after the training to tighten them up and make it clearer that the chair works for the board. Now we're all on the same page: everyone feels strongly that the staff works for me, and I am responsible to the full board."

A Change of Direction

So how does Principle III play out for Life with Leukemia? Carly's desire to support Sherri and protect her position springs from a genuine desire to help her friend in a time of need. But despite her well-intentioned motives, Carly is unknowingly injuring the board/CEO partnership and diminishing the worth of the services Life with Leukemia offers to the cancer community.

Ironically, Sherri is the first to realize it. If she is honest with herself, she knows that many of Life with Leukemia's services have suffered as a result of the difficulties she's experiencing in her personal life. She loves the organization, but she also realizes that it deserves more than she can give right now. The point of a nonprofit organization is not to create or sustain jobs. The beauty of nonprofits is that they are designed to fill a need—teach children, feed the homeless, and so many other admirable aims. Life with Leukemia is not about what's best for Sherri or how she can keep her job. It's about unselfishly serving cancer patients, survivors, and their families.

After much deliberation, Sherri thanks Carly for her kindness, expresses her sincere gratitude to the board for such an incredible experience, and resigns her position as CEO.

Carly is grieved by her dear friend's decision, but she understands the reasoning behind it. So instead of letting Sherri's departure derail the momentum they've already gained, she decides to do something her friend would have wanted.

Sherri passionately believed that the Six Principles model would be a real culture changer for Life with Leukemia. So Carly makes the decision to pick up the torch. It's time to introduce the Six Principles model to the board—especially now that they'll be looking for a new CEO.

Principle IV

The Board Creates Committees to Help Accomplish Its Own Job, Not the CEO's

January-February

The Program Committee Assumes Control

After the recent departure of Sherri Talbot, the Life with Leukemia board begins looking for a new CEO. And while everyone recognizes this as an opportunity for new life and growth, the staff and many of the board members are feeling a little lost without anyone at the helm. In fact, the whole organization is in a state of flux.

In the meantime, one of Life with Leukemia's programs starts to suffer. The Soul Foods program, which is designed to deliver both nutritious food and uplifting entertainment to bedridden leukemia patients, is floundering. Soul Foods has long been one of the nonprofit's most successful programs, but it's fast losing momentum and funds—so much so that the board's program committee is beginning to panic.

At the heart of this committee is Lori Whiten, the retired president of an area hospital. Lori has previously served one term as a board chairwoman, but since then she's really found her niche in the program committee. She's an extremely efficient individual, an energetic and committed board member who consistently donates substantial amounts of both time and money to the organization.

As one of the board members who originally suggested the Soul Foods program, the last thing Lori wants is for it to become defunct. So she makes it her personal goal to get the program back on track. She sends out a flurry of emails to Allan and Teresa—the other two members of the program committee—to orchestrate a string of meetings over a two-week period in which she introduces a new program outline, an ambitious fundraising strategy, and two new candidates for the Life with Leukemia program director. She also calls a good friend who writes for the local newspaper and talks him into putting out a press release to garner Soul Foods some much-needed publicity. The press release, of course, is written entirely by Lori—without running it by the rest of the board.

It doesn't take long for people to begin to talk. Board members are whispering among themselves, "Is Lori on the board or on staff?" And when she starts proposing new staff members to take over the program director's position, she's almost become an interim CEO, interjecting herself into hiring/firing affairs. Lori is acting in direct contradiction of Principle IV: the board creates committees to help accomplish its own job, not the CEO's.

Life with Leukemia is in a precarious position since, without a CEO, they're presently operating in a no-man's-land. Though Lori never meant to intentionally overstep her boundaries—on the contrary, she's earnestly devoted to keeping the organization and its programs afloat—under her leadership, the program committee has started to appropriate responsibilities and duties that really belong to the CEO. The bottom line is, board committees are created to support the work of the board, not the work of the CEO or the staff.

The True Purpose of Committees

When an organization enjoys a healthy and successful board/CEO partnership, there is a clear understanding that the board does not create committees to direct the day-to-day management of the agency. The CEO can, and indeed should, create committees, but these are staff-level committees, not board level. The Six Principles advocates a bold policy: any standing board committee that essentially duplicates the organization's managerial duties should not exist. Duplicative committees typically include program, personnel, and education. The development committee is the one exception—I recommend that nonprofits keep a development committee at both the staff and board level.

The committee culture presents a fascinating phenomenon. The whole purpose of committees is to enable the board to function more effectively; smaller groups make it possible for members to meet more frequently and discuss specific issues that often don't make their way onto the agenda for large group meetings. In theory, committees pave the way for focalized interest and superior performance of the board as a whole.

The trouble comes when standing committees begin to speak *for* the board instead of *to* the board. When Lori issued a press release in the hopes of drumming up community support for the Soul Foods program, she became a sort of de facto spokesperson for the board. When she presents her plans to redo the program, revamp their fundraising strategies, and replenish the program staff, she's meddling in management affairs. Ideally, committees exist to gather information that they can then present to the board so the board as a *whole* can make a decision. But Lori wasn't reporting back to the board; she was taking matters into her own hands. And the moment standing committees begin to do staff work, they've crossed the line between management and governance. In this scenario, the program committee divided the board, creating a situation where there was no longer one unified voice.

There are plenty of real-life examples of board members who decide to speak for the board. When Lori issued her press release, at least it didn't conflict with Life with Leukemia's official stance. I once saw a committee member at a press conference stating his individual position, which was in direct contrast to that of the board. We discussed in the last chapter how integral it was for board members to coalesce into one body; when an individual committee or committee member publicly voices an opinion that differs from the board's official stance on an issue, it undermines the board's authority and any perceived unity is shattered. A single committee member who speaks out of turn can compromise the whole board's duty to speak as a cohesive unit.

I've seen a number of committees break off from the board and coalesce within themselves to the point of exclusion. Some committees have their own conferences, their own bulletins, and they can even go so far as to distribute their own policies. When the program committee is saying this and the board is saying that, the CEO has to answer to a myriad of bosses—not to mention the staff members who are forced to do the same. When standing committees create additional bosses for the CEO, it compromises their commitment.

The Standing Committees Every Nonprofit Needs

At my seminars, I ask CEOs and board members to tell me which standing committee in their organization is the most infamous for getting into the management mix. Who's the most obvious culprit? Personnel and program committees are the two names that typically come up. If you think about it, it makes perfect sense. We've already discussed how a nonprofit's programs and hiring/firing decisions fall under the responsibilities of the CEO and the professional staff. And the easiest way to know which committees to get rid of is to look at the ones that duplicate managerial duties. Once you've adopted this outlook, it becomes clear that program and personnel committees are redundant and unnecessary at best, problematic and toxic at worst.

The problem with standing committees is precisely that: they just stand around. And when they stand around, they end up looking for little things, problems and issues that need to be fixed. I once did a workshop for an organization that held an event every three years, but the event committee met every month. I'm sure you know what's wrong with this picture! With meetings that frequent, the event committee is bound to veer into the more managerial concerns of the nonprofit.

Here's a powerful secret: committees for the sake of committees are not actually the problem. Every board will need to rely on committees from time to time. And some committees are useful and beneficial to the organization; there is no need to completely clean house and eliminate them all, which would be a pretty daunting task. The problem arises with the *type* of committees that exist in most boards. In the Six Principles model, there is an easy, two-pronged solution. The first part of this solution is to eliminate the problematic committees (personnel, program, etc.) and replace them with the standing committees you really need. Part two involves substituting a different kind of small-group structure for the committees you eliminated, using task forces and ad hoc committees instead.

First and foremost, let's take a look at the standing committees every nonprofit ought to have. The most important committee in the Six Principles model is the governance committee. This committee is responsible for:

- **G**overning
- **O**rienting
- **V**isioning
- **E**valuating
- **R**ecruiting
- **N**ominating

In short, it is the governance committee's responsibility to *govern* the organization it serves, leading the whole board in effective governance. They've always got their antennae up; for example, if the board starts to stray from Principle I, it's the governance committee's job to pull them back on track.

The governance committee supports the work of the board. It has existed in prior forms and gone by other names before. In fact a rudimentary version of it might already exist in your nonprofit's bylaws where it's known as the nominating committee. But the governance committee does much more than nominate board members. They must, for example, take responsibility for *orienting* new trustees. So many new board members are handed a thick governance packet and a copy of *Robert's Rules of Order* as the extent of their orientation. And does anyone ever really read board packets? Duty of care, duty of loyalty—what does it all mean, anyway? A dynamic orientation is so often overlooked, but it's fundamental for educating new trustees and making clear what is expected of a board member. The governance committee arranges and facilitates an impactful orientation that motivates new members, providing a sort of basic training and clearly informing them of their role on the board.

Next is *visioning*. While vision is a general board role, the governance committee can have a specific role; for example, they may be in charge of planning the vision retreat every three years. The governance committee is also directly involved in *evaluating* the board and the work of the board, which is covered in more depth in Principle VI. This committee also steps up to the plate when it's time to *recruit* new board members. Their responsibility is to profile the board, identify the expertise that will help move the strategic agenda forward, do the research on candidates that can support the board's growth, and present their recommendations to the board. And then there is *nominating*, which is self-explanatory: based on the results of their recruitment work, they nominate potential board members. It is not mandatory that the governance committee fulfill all of these tasks, but if they play an active part in orienting, evaluating, and recruiting, the board will be much stronger because of it.

After the governance committee comes the finance committee. The finance committee typically reviews the organization's numbers in greater detail than the full board. Since board members with little experience may get lost in overly detailed statements, it's the finance committee's job to highlight important financial trends and issues in a narrative report, presenting this information in as clear and concise a manner as possible so that the board as a whole is better able to respond. Ultimately, this committee must help the greater board understand the strategic implications of the budget. If you are a large nonprofit, I'd also suggest a separate audit committee; this is recommended by Sarbanes-Oxley and is generally a good governance idea, especially for organizations with budgets of more than a million dollars.

Since development is such an important role of the board, the third standing committee I recommend is the development committee. This committee oversees development and implementation of the Fundraising Plan, identifies and solicits funds from external sources of support, and works closely with the development director, if there is one on staff. However, keep in mind that the development director can potentially be caught between a rock and a hard place when there's conflicting advice coming from both the CEO and the development committee. The duty of the development committee is to provide crucial support, not to become the second boss of the development director.

Because this can be a difficult balance to strike, there's a lot of burnout among development directors. I once knew a woman who was the development director for a major suburban symphony. She had just finished selecting the table cloths for their gala event when in ran the development committee chair, saying, "I wanted lime green table cloths. These are mauve!" Believe it or not, it's a true story. They had to reorder the table cloths because of the color. This kind of thing happens more often than you might think.

The Six Principles solution is to create a culture where the development director on staff feels very comfortable utilizing both resources; she answers to the CEO as an employee, but she should also draw on the development chair's reserves of the three Ws of the ideal board member— wealth, work, and wisdom—effectively utilizing the full talents of the board. I suggest that the development director serve as a kind of liaison, almost as a chair of the group. She should never feel like she's serving two masters. But if she can bring them together and use them to double the organization's development potential, then it's a win-win situation for everyone involved.

The final standing committee every nonprofit should have is the ESAT, a novel and ground-breaking committee that we'll discuss in more depth when we get to Principle V in the next chapter.

Unleashing the Power of Ad Hoc Committees

The second step to solving all your committee headaches is to instigate ad hoc committees or task forces. A task force comprises all the pros of a committee—they are a small group of people working toward a dynamic goal, are able to spend more time on an issue, and have an ability to bring specific knowledge to the board—without running the risk of creating permanent rifts and divisions. You can create ad hoc committees for research, bylaws, PR, building, events, or any other number of purposes. And while they can be supportive of staff work, the best thing about them is that when they've accomplished their objective, they simply dissolve.

Another exciting thing about ad hoc committees is that you can look outside the board for qualified members. Let's say Life with Leukemia was thinking about initiating a new cancer support program. Though this technically falls under the programs umbrella, it is part of a long-term strategy to improve services and reach more people. What if, instead of looking to the program committee, the board elected to create a special task force? They could bring in a doctor, other community members, social workers—the sky's the limit really. Suddenly there's a dynamic team of people, dedicated to researching and unpacking the issue, who can come back to the greater board with their recommendations. The board either adopts it or doesn't, and then that's it—they're done. The ad hoc committee disbands and everyone goes back to their business. They do their job, finish it, and then they no longer exist. That way you're not creating a bloated bureaucracy; instead, you're allowing the nonprofit to stay focused on its mission and the people it serves.

Still another advantage of task forces is that they can help invest new potential board members in the organization. You might invite a community member or businessperson to serve on a task force to give him or her a chance to watch how the board acts and participate without promising any definite commitment. It also gives the board a chance to see how well they work together. Instead of tossing new board members to the wind and waiting to see how well they do, it can be extremely beneficial to screen potential new members through an ad hoc committee first.

The Executive Committee

At this point, you may be wondering about the committee that's most commonly associated with nonprofits, yet it's surprisingly the most notorious for causing problems: the executive committee. The executive committee is something of a holy grail for many nonprofits, and it often occupies 25 percent of board space. The problems don't always stem from power-hungry committee members; most executive committee chairs are trying to do what's best for the organizations they serve. But this particular committee is beset with a host of problems from the very beginning—the executive committee seems to always have more access to the CEO than the rest of the board, which is not at all conducive to a successful board/CEO partnership. It drives a wedge down the middle of the board, dividing them between the haves and have-nots. By definition, it bifurcates the board.

Sometimes, maintaining an executive committee is inevitable, particularly when the board is large. When your board has more than thirty members, you'll need an executive committee. But you should know that your executive committee is your de facto board. If you are operating with a large number of board members when really only a fraction of them make the decisions, why not consider streamlining the number of trustees? I worked with a United Way affiliate that, over a period of time, moved from forty-five board members to fifteen and excised the executive committee in the process. In my experience, I've found that a board size of twelve to twenty is the ideal number—big enough to encourage diverse opinions and talents and to ensure that no individuals get burnt out, and small enough to come together as one body with a focus on governing the organization.

Larger organizations cringe when they think about getting rid of the executive committee and downsizing the board. "We'll lose some of our most high-profile members!" they say. My answer is simple: *your actual board needs to be small enough that every member can be involved and engaged.* So if you want to have fancy names on your board, then create a board of advisors.

You take them out once a year and throw them a nice dinner, but they're not your governing board. They don't need to be at meetings, which is fine—they usually don't want to be—and they can still support and contribute to the nonprofit. An advisory board can be large, but if your actual governing board is gargantuan, don't fool yourself: your board of fifty is not your board.

Of course, plenty of people will argue that the advantage of the executive committee is that work gets done quicker. That may very well be true, but at what cost? Any course of action that alienates board members is never a wise choice. While there are certainly advantages to maintaining an executive committee, the disadvantages far outweigh them. I was once asked to shadow a board meeting of a nonprofit that had recently added a new board member. The new member, a head of a successful company who had showed great initial promise, was completely unenthusiastic and uninvolved. "Why isn't Alex engaged?" the board chair asked me.

After just one meeting, I knew exactly why Alex wasn't engaged. Everything got done in the executive committee, and Alex knew it. His initial passion for the nonprofit's mission had dwindled when he discovered he was nothing more than a motion-seconder and a report-hearer—he was just there to rubberstamp whatever the executive committee decided on. In the process of jettisoning the executive committee, the board coalesced as a team, and Alex's voice became just as important as the others'. Over a year's time, he even became the number two giver of a very prestigious board.

Make Your Committees Work for You

Reworking your committee structure is a surefire way to revitalize your board. By eliminating standing committees which are duplicative of staff positions, such as program, event, and personnel, you'll ensure that your committees support the work of the board, not the work of the staff. The governance, development, and finance committees serve to support the board's role as directors, and the ESAT exists to support and appraise the CEO's performance on an annual basis. When specific board-level projects are required, task forces or ad hoc committees are established for the duration of the project. And to ensure that the board consists of one overall governing body, the executive committee will no longer function.

Below is a diagram developed for a nonprofit in the social services sector to help them revise their committee structure. As part of implementing the Six Principles model, this organization successfully terminated the executive, program, event, and personnel committees. They also chose to rename the executive director as the CEO to reflect a more accurate description of her responsibilities.

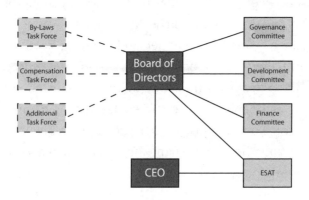

Principle IV is one that many of my former clients credit with changing the entire culture of their organizations. An area Red Cross chapter had a board of fifty when I first began working with them. Most of the board members were frontline volunteers, people who were responding to calls at three a.m. They were certainly a passionate board, but they did not focus on policy, and certainly not fundraising. Many just didn't see the need since the Red Cross is funded by United Way. The new CEO began shifting the paradigm when she joined the organization six years ago, but when she said, "We need to be raising money," the response she got was, "Oh no, we volunteer." When they decided to implement the Six Principles, it became apparent that downsizing the board was imperative.

Under the governance committee, the Red Cross was able to create a task force for streamlining the board. It didn't happen overnight. As the CEO noted, "You can't just read the book and say, 'Let's do it now.'" I met several times with the entire board, showed them what the process would look like, and worked a long time just establishing the steps we were going to take. When they finally adopted the resolution, they had created a three-year plan: in three years' time, they would be down to twenty-five board members. With one year left to go, they've actually made it to twenty-three, and the board/CEO partnership is functioning remarkably better because of it.

Restructuring committees was also important for the Red Cross. They had a committee for everything—volunteer, human resources, diversity, youth—thirteen standing committees in all. You can imagine how much time thirteen committee reports took up at a board meeting.

That was all they were doing! After they began using the Six Principles model, the CEO said that cutting down on committees "has probably been the most efficient thing in helping [them] keep more focused on what's important." They still have youth and volunteer committees, but they're no longer board committees. Now those interests are covered by staff and volunteer committees, and they're no longer a function of the board. Just because the board doesn't have a certain committee doesn't mean there can't be one in the organization. In fact, those committees are often much more effective when they're not an offshoot of the board.

The CEO of another nonprofit said, "Disbanding committees was a liberating act. There was a program committee that had become way too operationally focused. It wasn't at the strategic level, but was carrying out very low-level minutiae. I asked the staff, 'Are they a help or a hindrance?' And one of the first things we did was disband it." Initially, this choice to disband the program committee wasn't all that popular with the board. Many members felt that without the advice of that committee, the programs would be ruined. But concerned board members were gently reminded that that's why the nonprofit seeks to hire qualified staff. To set the board's mind at ease, an ad hoc advisory committee was formed that could be consulted when needed.

Schools have also reaped the plentiful benefits of Principle IV. William Broderick, the head of school of Fort Worth Academy, sings the praises of redoing the committee structure. He and the board run their school based on the goals in the Strategic Plan, and now as they're making decisions about what initiative is going to come next, they're able to form ad hoc committees that address those needs. The school enjoyed a recent triumph when they decided to form an ad hoc committee on wellness. They were able to tap into board members who were pediatricians and dieticians, as well as recruit other members of the faculty and parent body to serve as a part of the group for the extent of the year.

The wellness committee accomplished an amazing array of objectives: they arranged for portable defibrillators and CPR training for students and staff; they took a significant look at the food offerings of the catering service, successfully eliminating all trans fats and fried foods and making menu recommendations; they put incentives in place for weight loss and smoking cessation for faculty members; they reviewed the health and safety curriculum for students; and they restructured safety and security measures such as lockdown procedures. According to Mr. Broderick, "Over the course of the year, it became crystal clear that this wasn't the kind of work that you do once and stop doing." And while this was true, it was decided that this was not the function of a board of trustees. So after the ad hoc committee launched these wellness initiatives and generated a lot of excitement and enthusiasm for the program, it morphed into a staff group. The work is still going on, but it's no longer coming from the board. The ad hoc committee successfully shut down after a job well done.

The wellness committee was such a success story that Fort Worth Academy has applied the same technique to other areas. There was a parcel of land next to the school that's for sale, so they put together an ad hoc committee for property acquisition. They were able to pick people in the banking and land business, choosing from both on and off the board. That committee has been able to report back to the board with great accuracy and focalized attention, which is much more effective than what a standing committee without the same level of expertise could have done. They also just finished a three million dollar expansion, and while they were under construction for about a year, they put together an ad hoc committee that they populated with an architect, a contractor, and others—board members and constituent members who could speak the language. "If we'd been working under the old system," the head said, "it would have been, 'where does this fit?' But now we are able to create dynamic new task forces and committees on an as-needed basis. Restructuring the board like this has been highly effective."

At another school that adopted the Six Principles model, the education committee was posing a problem. It's a kiss of death for a lot of schools—all the things that should be handled by the head of the administration team, such as faculty review, curricular decisions, and other day-to-day concerns, end up on the agenda for the education committee. Instead of removing the education committee upfront, which would have upset many board members, they decided to take an intermediate step—they kept the committee but gave it an advisory role instead of a policy-making one. Since they were going to make some significant curriculum changes, they began looking to the committee as a group, which was comprised mainly of parents and people with connections to the school who could act as foot-soldier advocates. They contributed feedback and input, and when the board and executive made the curriculum change, the people on the education committee could be the grassroots spokespeople for it. This subtle change shifted the committee away from the policy-making role and got them into feedback mode. Instead of making recommendations, the committee presents research and gathers information. Eventually, they'd like to remove the education committee altogether, but for now this is a much happier median.

Life with Leukemia Hops Onboard

What happened at Life with Leukemia? More convinced than ever that it was time for a change, Carly seized the opportunity to introduce the new governance model. As they were discussing the Six Principles, something clicked for the board members, right around Principle IV. Lori raised her hand and very candidly acknowledged that she could see how her behavior was jeopardizing the governance culture; she also admitted that she was totally exhausted from juggling too much and expressed relief at the thought of being able to step back and take a breather. After they took fifteen minutes to discuss Principle IV, it was Lori who suggested creating a dynamic task force to revisit Soul Foods and see how the program could be salvaged—or if perhaps it was time for a new program to be initiated by the staff.

Excited by the potential of temporary committees, Life with Leukemia seized this opportunity to form another ad hoc committee—this one to interview possible candidates for the CEO position. It only took the task force one month of intense and dedicated work to find their next CEO, a remarkable leader and visionary. The whole board felt enthusiastic about the choice of Megan Jaster, and the committee happily disbanded after a job well done.

The other board members, impressed at how the Six Principles model laid things out so clearly, made the unanimous decision to bring me in for a seminar. Though they felt their schedule for the next six months was too full, they set a date for mid-August. My partnership with Life with Leukemia was about to commence.

Principle V

The Board Evaluates Its CEO through an Executive Support and Apprasial Team (ESAT)

March-August

The ESAT Changes the Culture

As Megan Jaster begins her tenure as CEO of Life with Leukemia in March, the board couldn't be more pleased. Megan is an excellent communicator and delegator. She recently relocated to the area after leaving a small hospital in a neighboring state, and everyone from her previous nonprofit raves about her high level of commitment. Her warm personality and great relations with people is what landed her the job.

So Megan sweeps in and redefines Life with Leukemia to reflect a genuine focus on the human aspects. She's able to restore the flagging morale of the staff, many of whom felt lost under Sherri's recent inaccessible leadership. She's keenly interested in establishing a productive partnership with the board and works hard toward that end. Megan is also incredibly excited about the Six Principles seminar in August; she hopes to shift the governance model to the forefront of the organization.

There's only one problem: the seminar is six months away. And even though the board has experienced great success with Principle IV, no one's there to instruct them on Principle V: the board evaluates its CEO through an Executive Support and Appraisal Team (ESAT). At the heart of this principle is establishing a positive and ethical method of evaluation for the CEO.

The consequences of this oversight don't reveal themselves immediately. At first, everyone is thrilled with Megan's personable approach, and things are going incredibly well for Life with Leukemia. The board meetings between February and July are an absolute lovefest filled with high fives, high spirits, and even a few hugs. Yet an eight hundred–pound elephant is lurking in the boardroom. Megan has all the people skills, but she's really never fundraised before and is spending all of her time engrossed in building internally. Out of politeness, nobody wants to talk about fundraising—but this kind of politeness is a lethal, paralyzing kind. The more people continue to dance around the issue, the more the problem continues to fester and grow.

In August, six full months have gone by, and fundraising hasn't been mentioned once. The board decides to evaluate Megan after her first half year with the organization. This meeting has a decidedly different feel. Allan takes Megan to task for shirking her duties as a fundraiser. Teresa echoes Allan's comments. Carly, the chair, while a staunch supporter of Megan, can't disagree with the evidence. Megan walks out of the meeting reeling from the stinging evaluation, rethinking her decision to accept the position. "Why couldn't they have told me this was a priority early on?" she thinks to herself, feeling like she's failed in her duties as a CEO.

The Three Most Common Errors of Executive Evaluation

What happened at Life with Leukemia was a classic case of backward evaluation, or evaluation in hindsight. When this happens, CEO evaluations are reduced to Monday morning quarterbacking between board members—they look back and say, "Let's figure out what went wrong and establish an evaluation based on that." Sadly, it's a problem that befalls many nonprofits. Not once did the board outline their expectations to Megan in advance. Naturally, somewhere in Megan's job description are some generalities about fundraising. But a dusty job description is not enough, because it's barely read at the first interview, if at all. Megan may have been evaluated on a key role, but it was one that was never specified, in writing or even verbally. And while legally this could be a perfectly valid form of evaluation, ethically, it is not.

Backward evaluations aren't the only kinds that cause problems. In my work with nonprofits, I've witnessed two other unacceptable ways evaluations are handled. I once got a call from a CEO shortly after her evaluation by the board; she wanted to discuss the evaluation with me. We met up at Starbucks, and I asked her how it had gone. "Well, it was pretty awful," she said. "I was brought before the 'tribunal' and they told me I wasn't professional enough." This was a woman who always dressed well and had impeccable credentials, so I asked her what she thought they had meant.

"The truth is," she said, "something happened three weeks ago that I think had something to do with it. One of the board members was strolling through the hallway, and she knocked on my door and kind of invited herself into my office. She was picking up different things in my office and was looking at all the stuffed animals on my shelves. Then at the board meeting she said my office was too cluttered and didn't give a professional look, and wouldn't you know it, this crept into her evaluation and onto her performance review. But I have to tell you, Jonathan," the CEO said as she leaned in over her latte, "I run a children's advocacy center. What do they want me to do? Take away all the stuffed animals, all the warm, inviting things for the kids and bring in corporate, sleek marble furnishings?"

This CEO had suffered from what's called an anecdotal evaluation—an evaluation based on an anecdote or some other little thing. I know a CEO who once received an uncomplimentary evaluation because she was running through the hallway to deal with a crisis situation and didn't stop to smile at a board member; because the board member felt insulted that the CEO didn't stop to say hello, it bled over into the evaluation that she was insensitive and impersonal. Anecdotal evaluation is a skewed system of judgment and is simply not ethical.

Another example: I once worked with a man we'll call Chris, the CEO of a New England nonprofit who had been there for three years without being evaluated. Finally he asked his board chair, whom we'll call Bill, when he might expect an annual appraisal. So Bill asked his company's HR team to design a survey to be sent to the board members and staff. Excited by this inventive approach, Bill marketed the survey with gusto and received a healthy number of responses.

Of course a "healthy number of responses" is not entirely accurate. Some people received the survey and quickly jettisoned it. "Chris is amazing," they thought. "There's no need to send this back." Meanwhile, a veteran staff member who had outlasted several former executives seized the opportunity to share his opinions about the "young Turk in the CEO's office."

The next board meeting was a spirited one, where the surveys were read while the secretary assembled the key outcomes. Included in the findings were comments about violations of staff dress code, ants in the break room, and unreturned emails. After the executive session portion, Chris was called in to hear the laundry list of complaints. A shell-shocked Chris left the meeting thinking, "Is this the type of evaluation I had asked for?"

Boards often succumb to the allure of surveys, which almost always lead to anecdotal evaluations. So often, a board sincerely looking to fulfill its duty to evaluate the CEO, sends out an unscientific, often hastily prepared survey. Rarely do surveys portray an accurate picture of the CEO's performance, and they are almost never tied to written goals. Instead, surveys present tangential evidence of the CEO's duties.

SPAN AND THE 360 SURVEY INSTRUMENT

A 360 instrument, which is a business form of evaluation in which a person is evaluated from all degrees by a sampling of different people, may seem to give an objective evaluation, but it can easily become a fishing expedition if no parameters have been established.

Oftentimes, these types of surveys degenerate into nothing more than popularity contests, which accomplishes nothing in the way of helping the organization meet its goals.

However, the 360 survey can be performed as a supplement to the SPAN system, which is discussed on page 73.

The third way evaluation is done incorrectly is simply not to evaluate at all. Sometimes board members don't want to cramp a CEO's style. I once received a call from a board member of a Midwestern boarding school that had gone through three heads[2] in seven years. He was perplexed as to why the school was losing students on a yearly basis. I asked him what process for head evaluation was used, and he told me, "We don't really have a formal process. Why is that relevant to the kids?"

It's relevant for a number of reasons. When heads are not evaluated, several things happen: One, goals are not being

---

2. The head in a private school is equivalent to the CEO in a nonprofit.

set and standards are not being met, which results in ripple effects throughout the schoolhouse. Two, lack of evaluation is directly related to turnover of heads, which in turn leads to an unsettled and disharmonious school community. When a head is replaced, usually two years of progress are lost. The final year (assuming the head received advanced notice) is generally a stagnant, lame-duck year. Then, the first year of the incoming head is a year of assimilation; significant changes generally do not occur. These two pivotal years can wreak havoc on the school's culture. And while it is inevitable that heads will change, how unfortunate when those changes are unnecessary, or worse, unethical. Backward, anecdotal, and shirked evaluations all put a significant dent in the board/CEO partnership and weaken the ties between the two arms of any nonprofit.

The Executive Support and Appraisal Team (ESAT)

Every CEO deserves to have an evaluation that is proactive, one that starts at the beginning of the year and is upheld throughout. It's not rocket science, but a surprising number of organizations fail to put an effective evaluation system in place. A successful board/CEO partnership necessarily entails that the board conduct an annual appraisal of the CEO, based upon established criteria. High expectations of the CEO are laudable—as long as they're established beforehand. So how do you make it happen? This is where the Executive Support and Appraisal Team, or ESAT, comes in.

The creation of ESAT has proven to be one of the most revolutionary concepts in the Six Principles model. Why do you need an ESAT? Interestingly enough, if we were to look at the bylaws of boards, we'd see that the board's role is to hire and fire the CEO. But if the board's underlying message to the executive is, "We're here to hire and fire you," it's not a very empowering position for the CEO, and it's certainly not a positive role for the board. What if the refrain were more along the lines of, "We're here to support and appraise you?" Now there's a message you can take to the bank.

The ESAT is the instrument that makes that happen. It's a standing committee, but we use the word "team" because it confers a very cooperative meaning, and the whole purpose of this committee is to support and appraise the CEO. Here's how the ESAT works: it's made up of two to three board members, the CEO, and one nonmember. The nonmember is an essential piece of the equation and offers a very unique advantage. If your bylaws don't allow for a non–board member to serve on a standing committee, you might need to tweak the ESAT makeup, but I'd strongly recommend that you consider adjusting your bylaws instead. Having a nonmember on the ESAT adds a lot of objectivity to the process.

Of course, this doesn't mean that you should go pluck a stranger off the street who's never been associated with your nonprofit. Rather, you bring in someone who's connected to the organization and its spirit—for example, a past board member. The CEO of a similar but noncompetitive organization, with a comparable budget, is another ideal option; he or she will be able to contribute an invaluable perspective. Another possibility is somebody who served on a task force or someone who is a sibling, parent, or child who received services from your nonprofit and feels motivated. The nonmember should have his or her finger on the pulse of the organization. It's got to be someone who realizes the importance of the nonprofit, believes in its services, and really has his or her ear to the ground; It can't be a yes-man. In fact, none of the ESAT members can be yes-people. Certainly they should be constructive and able to praise when praise is deserved, but they also have to be able to speak up when needed and eschew politeness and critique when necessary. They need to be able to pick up the phone and say, "Megan, are you aware of this? There are some rumblings; therefore, we should get together to discuss these things." A successful ESAT has the remarkable ability to nip problems in the bud before they fester.

The ESAT typically meets three or four times a year, although it's often helpful for the committee to meet once a month at the beginning, just to get things up and running. Their mission is simple: to craft a workable CEO support system where there's an evaluation from the get-go. The evaluation is based upon established criteria contained in a strategic appraisal document. Now it's time for another acronym—the Strategic Performance Appraisal & Navigation (SPAN) document.

Strategic Performance Appraisal and Navigation (SPAN)

The SPAN document contains annual and long-term performance goals, is based on a nonprofit's annual agenda, and is rooted in its mission. It is the basis for the periodic and annual review of the CEO. SPAN is a simple but incredibly powerful tool. It's a three-tiered process, starting with the CEO, worked through by the ESAT, and approved by the board as a whole. It's also broken down into three parts: Pre-appraisal, Navigation, and Appraisal. Pre-appraisal lays the groundwork, Navigation outlines how to get there, and Appraisal occurs afterwards to see if the goals were met.

Below is an example of the basic questions used to construct a CEO SPAN document.[3]

SPAN
STRATEGIC PERFORMANCE APPRAISAL & NAVIGATION

PRE-APPRAISAL
- Mission to Vision
    - Why am I here?
    - What am I passionate about?
- Strategic Roles
    - Which roles are relevant to the annual agenda?
    - What are the big rocks in my administrative arena for the year ahead?

NAVIGATION
- Goals
    - What are my four major, prioritized goals for the year ahead?
- Steps
    - What specific steps do I need to take to reach my goals?
- Criteria
    - How will I know when I get there?

APPRAISAL
- Successes
    - In which areas did I achieve my objectives?
- Modifications
    - Which goals need to be tweaked or carried over for the following year?

---

3. The full six-page CEO SPAN document can be found in Appendix A.

Creating the SPAN document works as follows. Initially, it begins with the CEO. The basic idea is for the CEO to lock himself in his office for a day, a weekend, or maybe even head off to the wilderness for a few days—somewhere with no phones and no computers—in order to take a step back and think. He should reflect on why he is with the organization, what he's passionate about, what roles of his are relevant to the agenda at hand, and contemplate any big rocks that lie ahead. This can be time-intensive, but it is absolutely worth it. After the CEO has brainstormed, he should cull the three or four goals that he is most passionate about. That's the Pre-appraisal part of the process.

Next comes the Navigational phase. This is where the CEO puts all the tough things down on the page—goals, steps, and criteria. You'll notice that the CEO is only asked to come up with four major goals. The old adage holds true: less is more. I've seen a plethora of CEO job lists, and some of them are crazy. Who can follow a list of eighteen different goals with sixty-five bullet points? There will always be a number of smaller goals, like setting the schedule for the week. But when it comes to the big-picture issues, I strongly recommend boiling it down to four or even three major goals for the year ahead. Some criteria for those goals are easier to quantify than others; for something like fundraising, all that's needed is a simple statement like: "I need to raise x amount of dollars." For a goal such as boosting staff morale, it's a little more delicate. Here you could do a survey specifically measuring the staff culture. Just be sure it doesn't turn into a thousand questions about how you like the CEO—that's just asking for axes to grind.

After the CEO has established his goals and proposed steps to achieve them, the ESAT schedules its first meeting to go through them. This is when the team gets into the nitty-gritty, discussing the CEO's goals and working to revise and revisit them if need be. For this part of the process it can be extremely helpful to obtain the services of a consultant, someone to oversee the process and make sure the team stays on target. There are nonprofits that have adopted the Six Principles after hearing the seminar, but without guidance, they floundered when it came time to put a SPAN document together. In such cases, even in the midst of an ESAT meeting where they were discussing the CEO's goals, the elephant stayed in the room. The teams deliberated on issues such as bringing in new computer programs, and in the meantime, basic staff/CEO issues were completely neglected. Nobody wanted to talk about it. That's why it is crucial to have a guide.

The Navigation and Appraisal parts of SPAN are fundamental for preventing situations like the one Megan experienced at Life with Leukemia. If there had been established goals during her first year as the CEO, you can bet that fundraising would have come up at the beginning of the process. And SPAN would have identified specific criteria for how Megan would know whether or not she was meeting her fundraising objectives. Then, assuming they had a functional ESAT in place, if something were to go wrong midyear—say, Megan hadn't hit the fifty thousand dollar mark by April—they'd be able to meet, discuss the problem, convey the issues to the board as a whole, and switch gears to get back on track. Now, if there had been established goals and Megan just didn't deliver the goods, that's another matter. But it's not acceptable to have an end-of-the-year board meeting where the attitude is, "Surprise, surprise—we didn't get that goal done," when Megan's thinking, "*What* goal?" That scenario leaves everyone feeling raw and unhappy.

It's important to note that the responsibility for evaluating the CEO belongs to the board *as a whole*. The SPAN document should progress through a three-tiered process: it begins with the CEO, moves on to the ESAT, and ends at the greater board. And no one should be rubberstamping; there should be discussion and candid feedback at each stage. Even after the ESAT has revised the CEO's SPAN document, the board may change one or more of the goals. They may also keep them the way they are, or change a few details here and there before ratifying it. After all, the ESAT is in place for support and better communication, but it must always report back to the greater board lest it become like another committee with too much vested power. The ESAT is not intended to be another smoke-filled VIP room that shuts itself off from the rest of the board, nor is it a reincarnated version of the executive committee. The entire board must approve the SPAN document and be involved from the initial stages because it must have a buy-in for these major goals. It's absolutely imperative that there be a board-wide discussion of the CEO's goals at the very first meeting so that the nonprofit can proceed with clarity and understanding throughout the year and face no unwanted surprises.

The ESAT as a Culture Changer

Once an ESAT has been established, there's a system in place for people to bring up issues they may have with the CEO—a system that works much more effectively than calling up the CEO in the middle of the night. Now if a crisis comes up, there's a mechanism in place. As the CEO of an association of over one hundred affiliates put it, "With the ESAT, the evaluation is no longer a once-a-year, have-to-get-this-over-with type of thing. It's an ongoing dialogue between key people and the CEO to take the temperature throughout the year." Yes, the ESAT involves a sizeable time commitment and often entails extra work. But in general, people who are invested in the organization want to be on this team. The ESAT is typically populated with good people and great board members because it's an exciting way of really seeing change.

The ESAT system can be a real culture changer for nonprofit boards. In my experience, I've found that the most neglected and misunderstood piece of governance is CEO evaluation. Typically, boards are intimidated by evaluations, often because they don't know how to handle them. Principle V of the Six Principles establishes objectives in a more holistic way, through conversation and give-and-take. Goals are formatively appraised, tweaked, and when necessary, shifted through the year. As the year comes to a close, the evaluation emerges. There are no surprises, no capricious demands, and no upside-down priorities. Rather, the CEO is answerable to predetermined criteria. Ultimately, this process does not remove accountability; it creates it. With an ESAT in place and a SPAN document on the table, a nonprofit can achieve utter transparency throughout the whole evaluation process.

Organizations consistently report real, tangible results after implementing the ESAT model. After I helped one nonprofit establish an ESAT, the CEO reported a substantial spike in recruiting affiliate memberships. In 2005, seven new member agencies were recruited, bringing in $5,250. In 2006, fifty-six new member agencies were recruited, bringing in $42,000. That's an 800 percent increase over the course of a year!

A school head at a private school where I consulted reported astonishing results in new family recruitment. In 2005, they had recruited sixteen new families and twenty-nine new students. In 2006, that number jumped to forty-nine new families and one hundred and four new students—a 300 percent increase.

Time and again, I've watched as the fifth principle completely revolutionizes the governance culture of an organization. And it's such a simple principle to adopt! Cindy La Porte is a school head whose institution has reaped untold benefits from implementing Principle V. After I conducted Trustee Training at All Saints' Episcopal School, a private school in Austin, Texas, Cindy asked me back the following year to train them in how best to use the appraisal tool. We were able to successfully initiate an ESAT consisting of Cindy; the current board president, Mari; the former board president, Carolyn; and a former trustee named Amanda. We began by going over the directions for how to use the tool and then set a date for the four of them to get back together.

In the past, the trustees had gotten together as a large group every March to discuss how well or poorly the year had gone, with each contributing something. Later, one of the trustees would transcribe the discussion, placing the comments under a variety of categories and then distributing a printed copy for all the board to review. They came back together in April to determine which statements actually warranted further discussion and which should just be dropped. An evaluation of Cindy was written, and one or two trustees shared the information with her in June. And while the evaluation was generally complimentary and included suggestions for improvement, she never knew in August what they were going to base her evaluation on in March, which is exactly why she wanted to use the Six Principles SPAN tool.

"Completing the Pre-appraisal and Navigation sections required more time and effort on my part than I *ever* imagined," Cindy said, "but it was an invigorating process. I used our Strategic Plan for guidance and then in the end, wrote my three goals, the steps with a timeline, and criteria to determine whether the goal had been met. Mari, Carolyn, Amanda—[my ESAT members]—and I got back together and discussed *every* page and every part of the process. I *wanted* them to know what I was passionate about, what I thought my job was, what was of significant importance to me, what I would like to see improvement in, and what I was honestly interested in doing. It was a lively conversation, and I shared with them my hopes and dreams in a way that previously I had only shared with my husband and two best friends. This committee now knew what frightened me, what excited me, what was difficult for me, and what was easy for me. And they understood better how goal-driven I honestly am, how important it is to me to do my job well, and how hard it is for me to stop working at the end of the day when there is still much to be done."

After establishing the strategic appraisal document, the ESAT met formally and informally a number of times throughout the year. For the first time in Cindy's eight years as head of All Saints' Episcopal School, she had the opportunity to know *in advance* what her evaluation would be based on, because she had the power to help create it. Not only did she get a substantial raise but also the largest merit bonus that she had ever received. And All Saints' had the benefit of a focused head of school who, because she was not worried about her evaluation or lack thereof, could devote more time to making sure the students were receiving the very best.

SPAN goals need not be confined solely to the professional realm. Mark Desjardins, another school head, believes that setting personal goals is equally important to his performance as head of Holland Hall in Tulsa. Part of Mark's SPAN includes maintaining some sort of fitness routine four or five days a week. "It's important to be able to articulate those goals to the board," Mark says, "and then hold yourself accountable to those as much as you can." How does maintaining a fitness regimen affect Mark's ability as a school head? That's easy—keeping those goals helps Mark stay in top shape, both physically and emotionally, which makes him better equipped to lead Holland Hall.

The ESAT Comes to Life with Leukemia

How did Megan handle the backward evaluation she received from the Life with Leukemia board? As the new CEO, she understandably felt a little uncomfortable about waving the Six Principles in front of the board with a big red circle around Principle V. Fortunately, outside assistance was already on the way—my Six Principles seminar was scheduled for the next week.

At the seminar, I worked closely with the board to help them develop a fuller understanding of each of the principles. As I presented the Six Principles, they participated enthusiastically, delving into the hands-on training with boundless energy. The material was clear, practical, and uplifting, and I could feel the excitement building as the seminar progressed. When we got to Principle V, the board saw the need for a more in-depth look at executive evaluation; they decided to call me back in for an intensive ESAT workshop a few weeks later.

Life with Leukemia has now established an ESAT with Megan, Teresa, and Carly. For their nonmember spot, they've asked Sam, a community leader who sat on the board six years ago, to join the team. Sam is intimately acquainted with the organization's history, but he's been far enough removed for the last few years that he's able to bring a fresh pair of eyes to the ESAT process. Now, with a SPAN document fresh off the press, they're off and running toward a changed culture and brighter tomorrow.

Principle VI

The Board Conducts Its Own Annual Self-Appraisal

September

The Board Looks Inward

Life with Leukemia is back on track. The governance culture has never been healthier, and the board is enjoying a period of great prosperity, especially since the implementation of the ESAT. Megan feels supported in her role as CEO, and the rest of the committee is excited to be part of a team that's enacting real change in the

*organization. Nobody's missed the program committee—
especially Lori, who's enjoying her free time to address the
agency's strategic needs. In the absence of the executive
committee, the governance committee is operating in full
swing. It's as if the tenets of the Six Principles model have
finally become engrained in the way the board and CEO
interact with one another, and a powerful partnership has
emerged. The times when the board members have to
take a peek at the Board Engagement Matrix are now few
and far between. The distinction between governance and
management has started to become second nature to the
entire Life with Leukemia crew.*

Forming the ESAT did something else to the Life with
Leukemia board: it changed everyone's attitudes toward
evaluation. Board members used to feel threatened by
the mere mention of "evaluation." But now that they've
wrapped their heads around it, they're feeling more
comfortable with the idea. So comfortable, in fact, that
they're ready to start talking about the sixth and final
principle of the Six Principles model: the board conducts its
own annual self-appraisal. It's time for Life with Leukemia
to alert the community to its newly fortified commitment
to its mission and the people it serves.

The Board's Self-Appraisal

The board's self-appraisal is the last piece of the puzzle,
and it's an important one. The decision to self-evaluate
sends a powerful message to the community, including
foundations and potential donors; it reinforces the value

of continuous learning about governance, and it affirms the nonprofit's commitment—both fiduciary and mission-based—to the larger community. After the executive evaluation has been taken care of under Principle V, it's time for the board to turn their attention to putting a self-evaluating system in place.

Unfortunately, Principle VI is the one that most often is overlooked. Many nonprofit boards can easily see the need for evaluating their CEOs, but they drag their feet when it comes to an annual self-evaluation. For so many organizations, everything begins with the strategic plan, which is an all-consuming process. In fact, it's so all-consuming that sometimes the final step gets neglected: actually putting it into place. No wonder boards aren't very eager to embrace a self-evaluation when they feel they're falling short in carrying out their strategic plan. But actually, according to the Six Principles model, this attitude toward governance is backwards. If you as a board don't know how to operate or what you need to do, how are you going to create a strategic plan? Yet for most nonprofits, it's a well-known fact that the weakest link in governance is self-evaluation. As one CEO put it, "Everybody likes to evaluate other people. But they're not so crazy about evaluating themselves!"

Why self-evaluate? As a nonprofit, your organization exists to serve the greater good. When board members volunteer their valuable time and energy without being compensated, it sometimes instills a latent attitude of, "What more do they want from me?" The answer is: a lot more. If you're not there for yourself—monitoring your own behavior and progress—then you can't expect to be there for the people you're serving. Therefore, to hold the trust, you need a self-evaluation. Even boards that do a dynamite job evaluating the CEO often don't do a good evaluation of themselves. At best, there's a checklist of questions such as: *How many meetings did I attend this year? How do I feel about what I'm doing?* A cursory checklist like this doesn't really do or mean anything in the grand scheme of things.

A thorough and insightful self-appraisal, on the other hand, acts as a kind of compliment to the donors of the community. It sends a message that says, "We care about this organization, and we're doing our best to see that it constantly improves." Foundations and potential donors want to see that a board is taking itself seriously. Just showing up to board meetings is not enough. There has to be an external focus, and there must be an awareness of how the nonprofit is measuring up to it. It is precisely the fact that the experience of cancer patients and their families is contingent upon Life with Leukemia, for example, that makes it essential that the board examine and evaluate itself.

Board SPAN

The Six Principles method of board self-evaluation is essentially modeled after the CEO's strategic performance appraisal. But for the board's version of SPAN, instead of four major goals, each board member needs one stretch goal. Thus when you have fifteen board members, each director should have a goal. This doesn't mean that the board has fifteen goals total—there might be three to five goals, and each goal includes two or three board members. For example, at Life with Leukemia, maybe Allan's stretch goal has to do with fundraising: he's going to arrange eight asks from potential significant donors. Perhaps Teresa and Carly have decided that when they co-chair the benefit dinner this November, they're going to aim for an attendance of three hundred fifty—a hundred more guests than last year. Once each individual board member has filled out his or her own SPAN document, it is the responsibility of the governance committee to collect the goals and discuss them with the greater board at the beginning of the year.

In my work with nonprofits, I use a four-page SPAN document for the board's self-evaluation. Much like CEO SPAN, the document is broken down into three components: Pre-appraisal, Navigation, and Appraisal. Pre-Appraisal includes questions pertaining to mission and vision (the individual's raison d'être as a board member) and roles and responsibilities, specifically goals gleaned from the annual agenda or strategic plan that are relevant to each member's individual role. In the Navigation part, each board member delineates his or her stretch goals for the following year. Then the Appraisal section of the document outlines specific steps needed to reach those goals, accompanied by a timeline and criteria/benchmarks to be used for the purposes of fair evaluation. Every board member should give thoughtful, detailed, and honest answers to all the questions in each part.

To initiate the board's version of SPAN, a governance committee member meets with each board member at the beginning of the year to establish his or her personal goals. In their conversation, they ask questions like:

"What do you want to focus on? After looking at our strategic plan, what is the area where you most want to stretch?" Over the course of the year, board members will provide status reports. Then at the end of the year, they will meet again, and the board members will be evaluated on their individual goals. It's a powerful way to ensure accountability and a very healthy learning process. The governance committee members themselves are evaluated by other members of the committee, and the whole board emerges stronger as a result.

GOING FROM SIX TO FIVE

I've sometime seen situations where a board has been very comfortable and successful with their own evaluation, yet the CEO's evaluation has been the weak link. In those cases, it may work the opposite—the board's successful evaluation will motivate the CEO to be more receptive to the process. This is especially true for CEOs with a long tenure who have never been evaluated before.

Now that you've got the Six Principles model, you have a whole new way of looking at things. It offers an incredible opportunity to change the dynamic of your organization and strengthen your board/CEO partnership. That's all very exciting stuff. But here's a word of advice: take it step-by-step. If you don't currently have an executive evaluation in place for your CEO, don't do a board evaluation yet. First build your culture around a successful evaluation of your CEO, and develop some momentum from that. Maybe six months will go by, or even a year, before you implement a board self-appraisal tool; that's okay. Staggering the last two of the Six Principles can be a great idea. Implementing ESAT *always* has an awesome impact on an organization; I've never seen a case where it did not. Then after the culture changes, and once people feel good and see the magic of an effective evaluative process at work, board members will feel more comfortable and much less defensive about opening themselves up to scrutiny. When they feel that evaluation is a supportive process, it inevitably becomes more palpably appealing.

The Exciting Potential of Principle VI

Once your organization is in a position where it is ready to commit fully to Principle VI, there are all kinds of invigorating ways it can play out. Perhaps the most exciting thing about SPAN is that it doesn't have to stop with the board. In fact SPAN can give birth to a number of parallels. As a radical way to effect change in an organization, SPAN can be additionally used for staff and/or faculty. Every individual, from the executive assistant to the tenured faculty member, would benefit from the opportunity to put into writing their hopes, dreams, goals, and fears. It's really a brilliant mechanism: evaluating people based on standards they themselves have created, with a built-in support piece. What could be more ethical than that?

To illustrate this in my seminars, I show a clip from a little-known film called *The Browning Version*. Albert Finney plays an English boarding school teacher named Mr. Harris who teaches the fifth grade. After being there for twenty-five years, Harris has just been let go and is feeling rather disillusioned. Early in his tenure, he acquired a nasty reputation as the "Hitler of the fifth grade," and it's entirely justified—Harris is a stringent disciplinarian and was an absolute terror for the majority of those twenty-five years. Though a brilliant teacher, he just never connected with the kids. On his last day on campus, one little boy looks past his hardened exterior and, seeing a flicker of humanity, provides him with a simple gift. It's a magical moment in the film; Harris has a kind of epiphany where he thinks, "What have I missed out on over these last twenty-five years?"

If this were an actual scenario—and I've seen its real-life equivalent on numerous occasions—there should have been an intervention long before the heartbreaking final scene in the movie. In a perfect (and noncinematic) world governed by the Six Principles, the head would most likely observe one of Mr. Harris's classes after his first year or two as a teacher. This would lead to a conversation in which the head would candidly say, "Your brilliance is apparent, but you just aren't connecting with the kids." Then he'd suggest a professional development program or a mentor to work with Harris and help him figure out how to relate. After six or nine months, it's entirely possible that Harris would find a way to marry his brilliance with a real love for and connection to the boys he taught. The head would evaluate his class again and notice a marked improvement. Every student who walked through Mr. Harris's future classroom doors would be inspired, and he would leave behind a legacy of kids who loved and respected him.

Or, alternately, maybe he wouldn't. Perhaps even with outside help, Mr. Harris wouldn't change his attitude and would continue to disparage and frighten his students. If that was the case, the head would approach him and say, "You know, perhaps you'd make a great college professor or researcher, but you're just not a good teacher for ten-year-old boys." After the initial upset, Harris would be free to pursue a career in a position that actually suited and satisfied him, rather than staying for twenty-five years in a job that embittered and isolated him. And scores of students would find greater fulfillment from a different fifth grade teacher who hopefully understood them better.

But in the film, as is often the case in real life, there is no evaluation, no support, and no appraisal. Likewise, there is no thought for what's better for the students. For twenty-five years Mr. Harris could have been affecting kids' lives for the better, inspiring them to do great things, but instead he fosters an unhealthy classroom environment all that time until he is unceremoniously dismissed, leaving no legacy at all—except perhaps for his one student who dared to look deeper.

Governance as a Way to Meet People's Needs

This example gives a powerful illustration of the effects failed governance can have on human beings. At its core, governance is about meeting people's needs. It is not an abstract concept, and it doesn't rely on some complex model. It relates to not just you, not just your board, but to the patients, the homeless, the children, and the families that are being supported by the work of your organization. If there is not a sense of partnership between the board and the CEO, and if there isn't an evaluation to go along with that partnership, then how do you know you are meeting your goals? How do you know that those people who are homeless are getting the food they need or that the kids who need advocacy are getting representation? If we don't establish a workable system, years later we'll look back and reflect on what might have been. Isn't it much better to begin evaluating now, while there's still time to make a difference?

Many boards have traditionally used checklists for their self-evaluations. Instead of eschewing these altogether, I encourage nonprofits to use checklists *in addition* to their SPAN evaluation. One nonprofit I worked with added their own twist to Principle VI—at the end of every year, they give each board member his or her own report card. The card includes general questions—how many committee meetings did they show up to, how many board meetings did they attend, in what ways do they think they're engaged, and so forth. Then the governance committee takes them, removes the names, and at the first board meeting of the new year, they pass out copies of the reports. Since they're anonymous, there's no risk of name-calling or finger-pointing, but the board gets an excellent idea of whether or not they're on target as they commence a new year. It's a great way to keep board members accountable. The governance committee, of course, knows whose report is whose. If a board member gets an F in, say, attendance, then it may be time for the board chair or CEO to sit down with that person and ask, "Are you ready to become a real part of the board community, or is it time for you to move on?"

For a social services agency that was trying to downsize its bloated board, the installation of a self-evaluation tool had an immediate effect. A survey was sent to every board member, explaining that the organization was adopting the

Six Principles and that their new commitment was to focus on fundraising and stretch goals while downsizing to fifteen members. The survey asked board members to be honest about whether or not they thought they were engaged. Through self-selection, five members stepped down, people who knew they were not engaged at the level they needed to be—the nonprofit was down to eighteen board members, to almost where they wanted to be. They underwent the Six Principles training with the whole board and have since done a couple of refreshers, just to keep the model in the foreground of everyone's thinking. According to the CEO, it's led to some great conversations and progress.

Don Parker, the board chair of Gilda's Club in New Jersey, had his own praise for Principle VI. "The final component of Jonathan's plan is the board's self-appraisal. Ironically, we began our renewal process with a self-appraisal and now will institutionalize the process. The clarity of vision, purpose, and accountability that has been generated during this journey has resulted in a heightened sense of purpose and an elevated energy level among board members. In the end, the process felt like a renewal of marriage vows, characterized by the trust, candor, and respect necessary to sustain us well into the future."

The Nonprofit Secret

Once Life with Leukemia decides to implement Principle VI and begins evaluating the board, amazing things start to happen. Suddenly, the nonprofit is attracting some serious attention; the organization has rededicated themselves to their commitment to help leukemia patients and their families, and people in the community are taking notice. After setting a personal fundraising goal, Allan received a call just last week from his former business partner, a wealthy leukemia survivor who has pledged a quarter of a million dollars. According to the number of RSVPs, attendance at the annual gala event will be 425, far surpassing Teresa and Carly's original goal and almost doubling the number of people who attended last year— all thanks to both women's hard work and planning. Left and right, board members are taking great strides to meet their stretch goals.

Inspired by these landmark successes, other members are setting goals with gusto. The whole group has evolved and matured so much that everyone finds themselves looking forward to board meetings—they can't wait to contribute their own success stories about how they are adding value to Life with Leukemia. The board is even considering redefining their organization's mission to expand their services, extending them to a larger coverage area. And now that their governance is in top form, they've asked me to run their strategic plan for the following year. One of the major changes that emerged was the adoption of a one-year goal to implement SPAN for all the staff members. Jerry, the finance director, couldn't be more thrilled. When he joined the nonprofit he was flush with talent and idealism, but since his unpleasant run-in with Allan last year, he's been feeling discouraged and unsure of his abilities. Now that he knows he'll get to have a say in his own evaluation, his enthusiasm is back with a bang. He's got all kinds of ideas and can hardly wait to enumerate his own goals and work toward them with passion and commitment.

At the end of their last board meeting, Life with Leukemia took a few minutes to discuss all the ways their organization had grown over the last year. Every board member had something positive to contribute to the discussion. "When we started out, it was like herding cats," Teresa said, garnering a chuckle around the room. "But look at us now! Sometimes I don't know what happened."

"I know what happened," Carly piped up, leaning in with a grin. "The Six Principles did. It's almost like we found the nonprofit secret," she said to a chorus of nods.

And the Six Principles could happen for you too.

The Next Step

You now possess the secret to nonprofit success. The Six Principles model provides a simple but revolutionary tool that will revitalize your organization in ways you can't yet imagine.

Let's take a moment to recap by reviewing each of the Six Principles, how they played out for Life with Leukemia, and the ways they can revolutionize your organization too.

Principle I involves shifting the board's focus from management to governance, ensuring that every member's time and talents are being used to their maximum potential.

At Life with Leukemia, Teresa Thompson was expending valuable energies on the argument over the invitations for their yearly social event, while the invitations should never have been on the board's agenda in the first place. By making an active choice to govern rather than manage, your board will free itself to pursue more worthwhile endeavors. It's a simple principle, but observing it can have far-reaching results. Formerly tedious board meetings become fun, fruitful gatherings where meaningful issues are debated, discussed, and, when necessary, delegated. The Board Engagement Matrix can also be an invaluable tool in keeping your organization on the right track.

Principle II focuses on the board having one and only one employee: the CEO. Our friend Allan Jameson crossed the line when he started to go directly to Jerry the finance director to give suggestions and tips, and he later realized the error of his ways. Similar situations crop up at many nonprofits, especially when well-intentioned former volunteers join the board and begin to blur the line between governance and management. By accepting that the board's sole employee is the CEO, you'll streamline the board's focus and responsibilities. Concurrently, staff members will be able to attend to their duties without becoming confused; they answer only to their boss, the CEO.

Principle III hinges on a parallel concept: the CEO has only one employer, which is the board as a whole. While friendships between CEOs and board members can be wonderful and healthy, they should never entail special privileges for either side—like when Carly offered to protect Sherri's job while she struggled through a difficult divorce. This dilutes the professional relationship between the two branches of a nonprofit. It is equally unethical for the CEO to work for more than one boss. Your board should be a cohesive, smoothly functioning unit, creating a strong and unified presence in the community and cementing your firm commitment to the mission at hand.

In Principle IV we discussed the true purpose of committees: to help accomplish the board's job, not the CEO's. With Lori Whiten at the helm, the program committee of Life with Leukemia was sapping the board of its rightful authority. There's hardly a nonprofit in existence that doesn't have some committees that are unnecessary and ineffective. By revisiting your committee structure; replacing defunct committees with vital entities like governance, finance, development, and ESAT; and reexamining the role of the executive committee, you'll be able to achieve a whole new level of success. And don't forget the value of ad hoc committees and task forces. These add an explosive burst of energy to address a particular opportunity at hand, then either disband or morph into a staff committee when the time is right.

In Principle V we looked at the ESAT—the Executive Support and Appraisal Team. This system offers an ethical and highly effective, dynamic new way to evaluate your CEO. When Megan Jaster began her tenure with Life with Leukemia, there were no formally established measures of evaluation. As a result, nobody clearly spelled out their expectations in regards to fundraising. With an ESAT in place, these kinds of oversights and misunderstandings are a thing of the past. When organizations implement the ESAT system, there are *immediate* benefits—it's a true culture changer. The SPAN document allows the CEO to have a part in his or her own evaluation by making specific goals and following through on them. The three-tiered process ensures that the document begins with the CEO, goes to the ESAT, and finally is approved by the greater board.

And in Principle VI we examined the final piece: every board should conduct its own annual self-appraisal. By creating their own SPAN documents, board members are able to clarify their individual goals and responsibilities within the greater organization, allowing for greater productivity and the attendant excitement that goes along with reaching goals. When they began to evaluate themselves, the Life with Leukemia board started to experience landmark success—fundraising goals were met with gusto and the yearly black-tie event was a smash hit. By holding yourself to a higher standard, you'll be able to keep yourself better accountable to the community and the people you serve. Everyone who sees your organization in action will think, "Wow, they're really serious about their mission!" And when that happens, people will start to pay attention.

At this point you're probably thinking: "Sounds great. Sign me up for the Six Principles!" So what's the next step?

Actually, there are three. Below are the three actionable next steps for your organization to take in order to implement the Six Principles model.

Step #1: Plan a Retreat

Now that you've read and have a handle on *The Nonprofit Secret*, it's time to orchestrate an annual orientation and retreat. Holding a Six Principles retreat is an excellent way to create buy-in and consensus among all the members of the board. It can also be a whole lot of fun, not to mention a great way to bolster the relationship between your board and CEO. Once the Six Principles are unpacked, you'll be in the perfect position to discuss how best they can benefit your nonprofit.

Step #2: Restructure Your Board

Your next task is to reframe the structure of the board, making the formal decision to adopt the Six Principles and focusing on redoing the committee structure. One of the positive outcomes of a Six Principles retreat or workshop is that, when it's over, you'll have a written timeline of which actions you'll take and when. Many people are inherently suspicious of board retreats—they often entail a lot of emotion and excitement that's not backed by any tangible goal-setting or results. That's why setting specific, time-stamped goals is key. This is also the point where you take steps toward creating and launching the ESAT and constructing the CEO SPAN document (and you may choose to initialize SPAN for board members, staff, and faculty members as well). Once the ESAT is underway, you'll find that the forward momentum is positively contagious.

Step #3: Third Party Objectivity

The third step is simple, and it goes in tandem with the second step: establish third-party objectivity. We talked earlier about the importance of CEOs leading up, and it's true—most board members want direction. But the CEO must lead up in a very smart way. After all, board members are missing their kids' soccer games or a night at the symphony—they don't want to feel like the CEO is coming down on them for not doing things the right way. This is precisely why acquiring the help of an objective third party is so important. If you're a CEO, you run the risk of trying to be the prophet in your own city (or a prophet in your own nonprofit, perhaps); if you go into the next board meeting and say, "This is how we need to operate," you might tread on some toes. Board members are much more likely to listen to advice from an outside source. If a CEO brings in a consultant or a speaker, suddenly the board is listening to an outside opinion instead of feeling like the executive is telling them how to do their job.

NONPROFIT STEP-BY-STEP

Oftentimes, a board member or a CEO will request that I give a presentation on the Six Principles to the board as a whole. After the board members have seen for themselves how the model can change their entire governance culture, they're more than happy to move forward on it.

Then I typically do a board restructuring and an ESAT implementation, which takes a full day. Many boards choose to make it a two-day retreat and devote one day to strategic planning or visioning.

For boards that want to reap the benefits of sustained guidance, I continue to work alongside them, coaching them through the adoption of the Six Principles over the period of three months to a year. You don't have to do everything immediately. In fact it's unrealistic to think that you'll restructure your committees by tomorrow and have board self-evaluations in place by next week. All you have to do is start. Simply start building on these principles and the rest will come.

Start Today

The Six Principles model has brought a good deal of hope and excitement to nonprofits all across the country. If you are passionate about your organization's mission, if you are seeking a vibrant governance culture, if you want your nonprofit to grow and evolve and strengthen, if you have big dreams and aspirations, if you want to better serve the people in your community and improve the quality of your services, if you want to be the best nonprofit you can be—then the Six Principles is the right model for you. All you have to do is start. Simply start building on these principles and the rest will come.

Here's to your unprecedented success.

CEO SPAN
Pre-Appraisal

I. Mission to Vision

In this fundamental phase, answering these questions helps crystallize your professional raison d'être:

1. Why did you choose to be in your field?

_____

_____

_____

2. What are the qualities that attracted you to this organization?

_____

_____

_____

3. What areas of the organization's mission statement resonate with you?

_____

_____

_____

4. What is your favorite part of your workday/workweek?

_____

_____

_____

5. What would you like said about you at your retirement party?

_____

_____

_____

6. Now, from this list, choose the three that you are most passionate about:

1. _____

2. _____

3. _____

CEO SPAN
Pre-Appraisal

II. Strategic Roles

In ten statements or fewer, summarize your strategic roles, accurately reflecting your professional duties and expectations. You may use your job description or similar documents to help create this list.

❯ _____
      _ _ _

❯ _____
      _ _ _

❯ _____
      _ _ _

❯ _____
      _ _ _

❯ _____
      _ _ _

❯ _____
      _ _ _

❯ _____
      _ _ _

❯ _____
      _ _ _

❯ _____
      _ _ _

❯ _____
      _ _ _

Now, review this list with the Triple-I test: Place a check beside the role(s) that you deem to be of significant importance for the upcoming year. After, review the list again and place a check next to the role(s) where you would like to see improvement in the year ahead. Finally, place a check beside the role(s) for which you possess considerable interest.

Select the three roles that received the most checks, and list them below:

4. _____

5. _____

6. _____

CEO SPAN
Pre-Appraisal

III. Annual Agenda

List the major objectives of your organization's annual agenda from your strategic plan. (If your organization does not have a strategic plan in place, brainstorm with your ESAT to come up with this list.)

> _____

> _____

> _____

> _____

> _____

> _____

> _____

> _____

> _____

> _____

Now, select up to four goals that you perceive to be most relevant to your role as CEO:

7. _____

8. _____

9. _____

10. _____

CEO SPAN
Navigation

Based upon the three strands of vision, strategic roles, and annual agenda, you will now formulate your list of up to four prioritized, realistic, major goals for the upcoming year. This stage is performed in conjunction with your ESAT, to discuss, modify if necessary, and confirm your goals, steps, and criteria.

First, transfer items 1–10 to the list below and carefully prioritize them in order of importance. Prioritize them in ABC-123 form: A = high priority, B = medium priority, C = low priority. Then, prioritize each category (A,B,C) by level of importance. (1,2,3)

〉 _____
  _ _

〉 _____
  _ _

〉 _____
  _ _

〉 _____
  _ _

〉 _____
  _ _

〉 _____
  _ _

〉 _____
  _ _

❯ _____

— —

❯ _____

— —

❯ _____

— —

On the following page, list your top goals and formulate the specific steps you need to take to reach these goals. Make sure to include a timeline within the steps grid.

Use the template in conjunction with your current planning system. You may modify as you see fit, as long as you activate your set of Goals, Steps, and Criteria.

The final stage is usually the hardest part: establishing criteria so that you and your ESAT will know when you have arrived. These measurements assess your success in achieving your goals.

CEO SPAN
Appraisal

	Goals	Steps with Timeline	Criteria
1			
2			
3			
4			

The Six Principles of Successful Board/CEO Partnerships

Principle I
The Board Focuses on Governance, Not Management

Principle II
The Board Has One Employee: the CEO

Principle III
The CEO Has Only One Employer:
the Board as a Whole

Principle IV
The Board Creates Committees to Help
Accomplish Its Own Job, Not the CEO's

Principle V
The Board Evaluates Its CEO through an Executive
Support and Appraisal Team (ESAT)

Principle VI
The Board Conducts Its Own Annual Self-Appraisal

For further information about scheduling a
Six Principles workshop, retreat, or seminar, please
contact Jonathan Schick at 214.587.3960 or
by email at jds@goalconsulting.com.

Visit www.goalconsulting.com, where you can find
many more helpful materials and information.

About the Author

Photo by Holly Kuper

Jonathan D. Schick is the president of GOAL Consulting. He is a dynamic leadership consultant and nationally known speaker.

Having served as the founder of two nonprofits, and a consultant for hundreds of nonprofit corporations, Jonathan has built a track record of successfully guiding organizational growth and change.

In addition, Jonathan holds an appointment as adjunct professor at the University of North Texas and is a featured presenter at major conferences throughout the United States and Canada.

Jonathan earned his master's degree in Educational Administration from Boston College, along with a bachelor's degree in Human Resources Management.